The Chinese
in America

Recent Books in English by William L. Tung:

The Political Institutions of Modern China (1964; 2nd ed., 1968)

International Law in an Organizing World (1968)

International Organization under the United Nations System (1969)

China and the Foreign Powers (1970)

Revolutionary China: A Personal Account, 1926-1949 (1973)

The Chinese in America (1974)

ETHNIC CHRONOLOGY SERIES
NUMBER 14

The Chinese in America
1820-1973
A Chronology & Fact Book

by

William L. Tung

1974
OCEANA PUBLICATIONS, INC.
DOBBS FERRY, NEW YORK

Library of Congress Cataloging in Publication Data

Tung, William L., 1907-   comp.
     The Chinese in America, 1820-1973.

          (Ethnic chronology series, no. 14)
          SUMMARY: A chronology of the Chinese in America from
     1820 to 1973 with pertinent documents included.
          Bibliography: p.
          1. Chinese in the United States -- History--Chronology.
     2. Chinese in the United States--Legal status, laws,
     etc. [1. Chinese in the United States--History]
     I. Title.   II. Series.
     E184.C5T86   325'.251'0973   74-3116
     ISBN 0-379-00510-7

Manufactured in the United States of America

1827530

TABLE OF CONTENTS

FOREWORD

As one of Oceana's Ethnic Chronology Series, this book follows the series format by treating the history of the Chinese in the United States in three parts: (1) chronology, (2) documents, and (3) bibliography. The changing status of the Chinese in this country during different periods, classification of documents, and selection of bibliographical materials are explained at the beginning of each category. A brief review of the subject is presented in the Introduction.

Limited by prescribed space and specified format, the present work is designed not as an exhaustive study for experts but as a convenient guide for students and general public who are interested in this topic. For further references, readers are advised to consult the official and unofficial sources listed in the bibliography.

In preparing this book, I have obtained useful information from prior publications on the Chinese in the United States, particularly several recent ones by S. W. Kung, Betty Lee Sung, and Cheng-tsu Wu, to whom I wish to express my gratitude. For many valuable suggestions and comments, I deeply appreicate the generosity of Professor Raymond L. Carol of St. John's University, New York; Professor Ronald M. Schneider and Mrs. Roslyn Kaplan, my colleagues at Queens College of The City University of New York; and, last but not least, my wife Portia. I am, however, solely responsible for the facts and views presented herein.

William L. Tung
Professor of International Law and Far
   Eastern Studies
Queens College
The City University of New York

Jamaica Hills, New York

INTRODUCTION

The status of the Chinese in the United States has undergone drastic changes since the pioneer days. They were initially welcomed to meet the demand for cheap labor in the middle of the nineteenth century, but did not receive fair treatment legally or otherwise. During and after World War II, both Congress and the executive branch adopted a more enlightened view toward immigration and naturalization and gradually extended to the Chinese the basic principle of equality before the law. Although Chinese-Americans (Americans of Chinese descent) have not yet been appointed to cabinet or corresponding posts, opportunities in elective offices and non-political fields have now been opened to them despite some remaining prejudices.

It is difficult to ascertain the exact year when the first Chinese came to the United States. Certain historians described the presence of Chinese shipbuilders in lower California as early as 1571, Chinese laborers in the Far West in 1788, and one Chinese living in New York in 1807. Some informal sources went so far as to state the advent of the Chinese in North America and other regions of the Western Hemisphere even before the colonial days. Nontheless, the American Immigration Commission recorded 1820 as the year that the first Chinese came to the United States.

American information on the Celestial Empire immediately after the War of Independence derived essentially from European literature. The founding fathers of the Republic, including Washington, Franklin, Adams, Jefferson, Hamilton, and Madison had only vague knowledge about China and the Chinese. The first American traders reached China on August 28, 1784, when the Empress of China anchored at Whampoa, the harbor of Canton. The merchants were later followed by missionaries in the 1830's. But no official relationships were established between the two countries until the conclusion of the Treaty of Wanghia on July 3, 1844, by which Americans in China had long enjoyed a privileged status as the nationals of Great Britain and several Western powers through the application of the most-favored-nation clause. They were exempt from local jurisdiction under the terms of extraterritoriality, which was, however, not reciprocally provided for the Chinese government over its nationals in the respective countries.

The Chinese imperial code originally forbade expatriation, and violators were severely punished. Even after the official revocation of this law in the 1860's, Manchu emperors never encouraged emigration. Bound by national pride and social tradition, the Chinese gentry class generally frowned upon the idea of leaving the fatherland. It was not until the middle of the nineteenth century that Chinese from Kwangtung province began to come to California in large numbers, working in gold mines, on farms and railways. Their endurance and industriousness created a favorable impression upon their employers, but stirred up jealousy and enmity among white laborers, who frequently resorted to physical violence against Chinese lives and property. Reluctant to enter into full-fledged relations with foreign nations, China did not accredit permanent envoys to Washington and other capitals until 1878. Lack of diplomatic protection left the Chinese immigrants virtually helpless.

After the completion of the Transcontinental Railroad, the Chinese became unwanted. First, the state legislature of California passed a series of discriminatory laws and regulations against them. Then, beginning in 1882, Congress enacted several exclusion acts completely closing the door to Chinese laborers. It is indeed an irony of history that this land of immigrants should have imposed the harshest laws against the late comers. At the peak of legislative and administrative restrictions, even Columbus would have had difficulty entering the country.

In certain respects, early Chinese immigrants -- particularly the indentured, contract laborers, or coolies -- did not portray a good image of their country and people. Their strange attire, aloofness, and illiteracy generated suspicion and contempt among many Americans. But these poor sojourners were peaceful and contented earning enough money to maintain themselves and their families. Judging by their small number, the malicious slogan "yellow peril" was entirely without foundation. While comparatively underprivileged, they should by no means have been classified as an "inferior race," as arrogantly declared by some white people, whose ignorance of the history and civilization of others was responsible for assuming a sense of superiority just as the Manchu court once mistakenly took a disdainful attitude toward the early Western traders.

Although Sinophobia was initially caused by Chinese labor competition, American deep-rooted antipathy to color -- the Blacks and the Indians -- had also contributed prejudices against the first substantial group of non-white immigrants coming to the United States. Actually, the term "white" is a misnomer in its application to one's skin, because all peoples in the world are "colored" in the true sense of the word even though some of them, such as the Scandinavians, have comparatively lighter complexions. To many Caucasians, the assimilation of Chinese and other Asiatic races has been a cause of concern. Again, no race is unassimilable and the fundamental obstacle to the "Americanization" process is the discrimination by the majority against the minority. With the exception of the native Indians, all Americans are immigrants or their descendants. But to make America live up to its reputation as a "melting pot," different ethnic groups should be treated equally so as to work together harmoniously.

Ever since the outbreak of the Sino-Japanese War in 1937, the image and status of the Chinese in the United States have been gradually improved. Americans first admired the Chinese in their heroic resistance against foreign invasion, and then a spirit of comradeship between the two peoples developed after Pearl Harbor. The conclusion of a new Sino-American treaty on reciprocal basis and the repeal of all Chinese exclusion laws by Congress

in 1943 have not only strengthened the state relationship but also enhanced
the legal status and social prestige of the Chinese in the United States.
After the shift in power on China's mainland and the liberalization of American immigration laws in recent years, more Chinese, including many intellectuals and businessmen, came to this country, not as temporary sojourners but to become American citizens through naturalization.

According to the 1970 census, the number of Chinese in the United
States totaled 435,062. Among them are hundreds of scholars and scientists who have distinguished themselves in a variety of professions. Thus
the activites of the Chinese in this country are much broader now than those
of the early immigrants -- laborers, laundrymen, restaurant and small
shop operators. The accomplishments of many Chinese-Americans may
be found in Who's Who in America and other biographical publications; a
few of them are briefly described in this book for illustration. Having
made due contributions and shared equal responsibilities to this country,
the Chinese are undoubtedly entitled to the same rights and privileges as
Americans of other ethnic origins.

PART I

CHRONOLOGY

PART I. CHRONOLOGY

A study of the Chinese in the United States is closely related to the history of their immigration, which may be classified into four periods:

Free immigration (1820-1882), when Chinese labor was much needed for the exploitation of natural resources and construction of railways;

Discriminatory restrictions (1882-1904), covering the period from the passing of the first exclusion act on May 2, 1882, up to the enactment of the 1904 act;

Absolute exclusion (1904-1943), beginning with the act of April 27, 1904, which extended all Chinese exclusion laws then in force indefinitely and applied to all insular possessions of the United States, until the repeal of all Chinese exclusion laws on December 17, 1943; and

Gradual liberalization (1943--), achieved by several congressional acts after the repeal of all Chinese exclusion laws in December 1943, particularly the 1965 Immigration and Naturalization Act.

The following chronology begins in 1820 and ends in 1973. With a few exceptions in the first period, all major events are consecutively described every year. Whenever necessary and possible, months and dates are also indicated.

FREE IMMIGRATION (1820-1882)

1820   The Immigration Commission reported the arrival of the
                first Chinese in the United States.

1821-1840   According to the records of the Immigration Commission,
                ten more Chinese came to the United States during the two
                decades.

1844   July 3. The United States established formal relationships
                with China by the conclusion of the Treaty of Peace, Amity,
                and Commerce, signed at Wanghia. Among the unilateral
                rights and privileges obtained by the United States was ex-
                traterritoriality or consular jurisdiction over American
                nationals in China. No such reciprocity was extended to
                China over her nationals in the United States. (See Docu-
                ment 15.)

1845   December 31. The first Sino-American treaty of 1844
                came into effect by an exchange of ratifications at Canton.

1847   The first group of Chinese students arrived in the United
                States to receive higher education: Yung Wing, Wong
                Hsing, and Wong Foon. Their trip was sponsored by the
                Reverend Samuel Robbins Brown, principal of the Morri-
                son School at Macao. Because of ill health, however, Wong
                Hsing soon left for China. Both Yung and Wong Foon stu-
                died at the Monson Academy in Monson, Massachusetts.
                Yung eventually became a prominent scholar and educator,
                and also the first Chinese who obtained American citizen-
                ship through naturalization. He went back and forth be-
                tween China and the United States, and brought many Chi-
                nese students to study in American institutions. Perhaps
                no American or Chinese had contributed more to Sino-
                American cultural exchange than Yung in the early years.

1848   Gold was discovered at John Sutter's Sawmill, north of San
                Francisco. A group of Chinese laborers, two men and one
                woman, arrived in California. The men went to work in
                the mines, while the woman was employed at the home of
                Charles Gillespie, an American missionary from Hongkong
                coming back to the United States with them on board the
                Bard Eagle.

1849   The number of Chinese laborers in California reached fifty-
                four.

Yung Wing and Wong Foon graduated from Monson Academy in Monson, Massachusetts. Then Wong left the United States for Scotland and enrolled at the University of Edinburgh; Yung registered at Yale University, New Haven, Connecticut.

1850 The number of Chinese in California totaled four thousand by the end of the year. Their rapid influx was largely due to the demand for cheap labor in this new state. Natural calamity and horrors of war during the period of the Taiping Revolution (1850-1864) made many Chinese flee from Kwangtung province to Hongkong and Macao, where they were contracted by coolie traders and shipped to the west coast of the United States and other countries, particularly Cuba and Peru. Their industriousness, frugality, and willingness to undertake any kind of work pleased the employers but generated jealousy and antagonism among white workers.

The California legislature enacted the Foreign Miners' License Tax Law, under which laborers of Chinese descent and of some other nationalities were required to pay special taxes.

1851 There was a rapid increase of Chinese in California, from four thousand to twenty-five thousand within one year.

1852 The California legislature imposed a new tax of three dollars per person on foreign miners. Another law was enacted to enforce masters of ships to pay five to ten dollars for each passenger. More than twenty thousand Chinese arrived in San Francisco this year, contributing 45 percent of the total amount of this tax. In spite of the discriminatory measures passed by the legislature, Governor McDougal openly praised the Chinese as "one of the most worthy of our newly adopted citizens."

Miners in Marysville, California adopted a resolution denying mining claims to Chinese. In several other communities, Chinese workers were forced out of mining operations.

In Hawaii, the Royal Hawaii Agricultural Society imported 280 Chinese laborers.

1853 March 30. The California legislature passed An Act to Provide for the Protection of Foreigners, and to Define Their Liabilities and Privileges. It imposed special taxes on foreign gold miners, who were then largely Chinese. Because of the license tax and discovery of gold in Australia, only 4,470 Chinese came to the United States this year, barely offsetting the number of departures.

1854

There was again an influx of over thirteen thousand immigrants this year, when California suffered a business recession. White workers blamed the colored people, particularly the Chinese, as partly responsible for their unemployment and economic reverses.

The State Supreme Court of California ruled, in People, Respondent, v. George W. Hall, Appellant (see Document 18), that the laws of California prohibited all colored people from giving evidence in court against white persons. This ruling was affirmed in The People of the State of California, Respondents, v. James Brady, Appellant, decided by the same court this year.

April. The first Chinese newspaper in California, the San Francisco Golden Hills' News (Kim Shan Jit San Luk), was published.

The Chinese in California formed the Six-District Association for mutual help in the midst of American prejudices and discriminations. Almost all of the early immigrants came from six districts of Kwangtung province, each of which established its own organization: Kong Chow, Sam Yup, Sze Yap (later replaced by Hop Wo), Yeung Wo, Kipkat (later changed to Yao Wo), and Ning Yung (the largest in membership).

1855

January 4. The San Francisco Oriental (Tung Ngai San Luk), another Chinese newspaper, published its first issue.

April 28. The California legislature passed an Act to Discourage the Immigration to This State of Persons Who Cannot Become Citizens Thereof, whereby the master, owner, or consignee of any ship was required to pay fifty dollars for each of its passengers ineligible for American citizenship. (See Document 1.)

1856

December. The Sacramento Chinese Daily News was published, but it lasted only two years.

1857   In spite of racial prejudices, there were mixed marriages of Chinese men with Irish and German girls, as recorded in Harper's Weekly.

1858   April 26. The California legislature passed An Act to Prevent the Further Immigration of Chinese or Mongolians to This State. (See Document 2.)

During the course of Sino-American negotiations for the conclusion of the Treaty of Tientsin of June 18, 1858, an informal suggestion was made by an American representative to Viceroy Tien-hsian Tan that the Chinese government send consular officers to protect the interests of the Chinese living in the United States. The Chinese viceroy could see no reason to protect those who left the fatherland without permission.

1859   The Imperial government reversed its traditional policy by proclaiming that Chinese subjects could go abroad for permanent settlement. This occurred one year after the signing of the Treaty of Tientsin between China and several foreign powers, including the United States.

1860   The 1860 census revealed the total number of Chinese in the United States as 34,933. In the decade of 1850-1860, very few Chinese applied for American citizenship, but they soon realized its importance for re-entry to the United States after visiting China.

According to a California statute, Mongolians, Indians, and Negroes were excluded from public schools.

Chinese fishermen in California were required by law to pay four dollars per month.

1861   More Chinese came to California this year. According to the records of the Customs House of San Francisco, new arrivals were 8,434 and departures, 3,594.

1862   April 26. The California legislature passed An Act to Protect Free White Labor against Competition with Chinese Coolie Labor, and to Discourage the Immigration of the Chinese into the State of California. (See Document 3.)

Chinese in California over eighteen years of age were required by a police tax law to pay $2.50 per person if they had not paid the foreign miners' license tax.

1863   The California legislature enacted a law under which no
        Indian or person having one half or more Indian blood, or
        Mongolian or Chinese, could be permitted to give evidence
        in favor of, or against, any white man.

        When most of the white laborers working in the hills for
        the construction of the Central Pacific Railroad could not
        stand the hardships and quit their jobs, Charles Crocker,
        one of the Big Four partners, thought of recruiting Chinese
        laborers. His idea was successfully carried out in ensu-
        ing years.

1864   Chinese labor constituted a large part of the working force
        of four thousand for the construction of the Central Pacific
        Railroad, the white laborers numbering only one thousand.

        California's fishing tax law passed in 1860 was repealed.

1865   Impressed by Chinese laborers' successful performance in
        railway construction, the Central Pacific recruited more
        of them, first in California and later in Kwangtung. There
        were ten thousand Chinese laborers on the job at the peak
        of its construction. White workers first protested, but
        soon lost interest in the hard and dangerous conditions in
        building the railway through the mountains.

1866   Among the Chinese laborers working in the cane fields of
        Louisiana, some were brought over from Cuba.

1867   The naturalization of the Chinese had become one of the
        outstanding issues in California's state politics this year.
        White workers were afraid of the keen competition of the
        Chinese laborers, whose employment by the Central Pacific
        Railroad had then reached its peak. Labor groups deman-
        ded further legislation against Chinese immigration.

1868   July 28. The United States and China concluded the Addi-
        tional Articles to the Sino-American Treaty of June 18, 1858.
        It was signed in Washington, D.C., by Secretary William
        H. Seward (for the United States) and Anson Burlingame
        (for China). Generally known as the Burlingame Treaty, it
        recognized the right of free migration and emigration of
        the citizens of both countries, with the exception of naturali-
        zation. It also guaranteed their reciprocal privileges of

residence, school, and travel on the basis of the most-favored-nation treatment. (See Document 16.) As American
Minister to China, Burlingame had won considerable respect from the Imperial Court. After his retirement, China appointed him to head a diplomatic mission to the United
States and European countries, accompanied by two Chinese envoys, Chih-kang and Sun Chia-ku.

1868 When forty thousand Chinese miners were driven out by
white laborers on the west coast, they went to work on
farms and rendered household services, hoping to be left
alone without further molestations.

1869 The completion of the Transcontinental Railroad by joining
the tracks of the Central Pacific and the Union Pacific
marked one of the most important achievements in the
nineteenth century. When the construction of the Central
Pacific Railroad reached its last stage, Chinese labor constituted 90 percent of the working force of ten thousand.
However, the Chinese soon became unwanted in the West,
and even the enthusiastic attitude of the eastern American
leaders toward the use of Chinese labor began to shift.

November 23. The Burlingame Treaty of 1868 was ratified
by the United States and China at Peking. American hope
to carry on large-scale trade with this most populous country in the world surged.

Many Chinese laborers deserted the fields in the South and
settled in St. Louis.

1870 February 11. The Colorado legislature passed a joint resolution, welcoming Chinese immigrants "to hasten the development and early prosperity of the Territory by supplying
the demand for cheap labor." But this policy did not last
long, as evidenced by anti-Chinese agitation in Denver ten
years later.

Former Secretary of State William H. Seward arrived in
Peking and exchanged views with Chinese statesman Wên
Hsiang on the advantages of China's sending diplomatic
missions abroad.

While the construction of the Transcontinental Railroad
speeded the eastward movement of the Chinese, a small
number found their way into the South. About six hundred

took part in building portions of the Alabama and Chatta-
nooga Railroad in the winter of this year, and two hundred
fifty were employed by General John G. Walker for the
Houston and Texas Railroad. There was also an increas-
ing number of Chinese working on farms.

Chinese laborers arrived in Massachusetts. The shoe fac-
tory of Calvin Simpson in North Adams, Massachusetts
employed seventy Chinese boot and shoe workers. They
were generally welcome at the beginning, but some newspaper editors on the east coast started to advocate Chinese
exclusion.

California required other races to attend public schools
separate from the whites.

The number of Chinese in the United States reached 64,199,
most of whom resided in the West.

1871   Fou Loy & Co., a Chinese firm in New Orleans and San
Francisco, advertised to recruit fifteen hundred laborers
from China at twenty-two dollars per month. Several hundreds were employed by planters in Mississippi, Georgia,
Arkansas, and other states; many of them later left the
fields for other jobs at higher wages.

There was a massacre of Chinese laborers in Los Angeles.
Only the bravery of a few American individuals saved them
from total annihilation.

1872   July. Accompanied by Yung Wing, the earliest Chinese-
American scholar mentioned before, a group of thirty Chinese students, aged from ten to fifteen years, were sent by
the Chinese government to the United States. This was followed by three other groups in equal numbers in the suc-
ceeding years. All of them received higher education in
this country, and later achieved distinguished careers in
China.

July. Seventy Chinese laborers, who had just completed
grading the route of a projected railroad near New Orleans,
were employed by the Beaver Falls Cutlery Company in
Pennsylvania.

California prohibited Chinese from owning real estate or
securing business licenses.

The International Workingmen's Association held its first
convention in Cleveland and adopted a resolution calling for
"complete political and social equality for all, without distinction of sex, creed, color or condition." However, this
high-sounding principle failed to help the actual situation
of Chinese immigrants; nor did the Association's own attitude in the ensuing years conform with that resolution.

1873 The unemployment problem occurring in a year of economic depression had furthered the anti-Chinese movement.
The International Workingmen's Association advocated an
anti-coolie policy, which was, in effect, against the immigration of Chinese laborers. There was also some concern
among many Americans that the Chinese coolie might become a servile class of permanent nature.

1874 White unionized cigarmakers in San Francisco introduced
labels and certificates to call on the proprietors to sell
their cigars only, and not to sell or buy Chinese-made
cigars. This agitation was followed by white cigarmakers
in St. Louis in the following year.

1875 March 3. Congress passed an immigration act barring con-
victs and prostitutes coming to the United States. Since
the early state laws regulating immigration were all declared unconstitutional by the Supreme Court of the United
States, this act of 1875 was considered as the first one excluding the admission of certain aliens.

The anti-Chinese movement, started in California, gradually spread to other states, particularly Oregon and Washington. White workers found it increasingly difficult to
compete with the industriousness and endurance of the Oriental laborers.

For the promotion of friendly relations and protection of
Chinese nationals, the Chinese government finally appointed Ch'en Lan-pin and Yung Wing as Imperial Commissioners to the United States, Peru, and Spain.

1876 Many Chinese were forced out of small towns in California,
and some were violently attacked.

The Sinophobes in California extended their influence far
beyond the state. In the presidential election of 1876, both
political parties had to make concessions to them on the

issue of Chinese immigration.

1877   Sinophobes easily attracted the attention of political leaders
        at a time of labor unrest and general depression. This was
        the year when the Workingman's party of California was
        founded under the leadership of Denis Kearney, who was
        known for extreme racism toward non-white workers.
        Chinese houses and business premises were burned. In
        his report on the character, extent, and effect of Chinese
        immigration, Senator Oliver P. Morton of Indiana consid-
        ered racial prejudice as its real issue.

1878   April 1. California enacted an act to require the Board of
        Supervisors of the City and County of San Francisco to in-
        crease the police force and provide for the appointment,
        regulation, and payment thereof. But this act prohibited
        the provision of special police officers in that part of the
        city and county known as the Chinese quarter, the bounda-
        ries of which were to be established from time to time by
        police commissioners.

        September 28. The Chinese Imperial Commissioners pre-
        sented their credentials to the United States government,
        two years after their appointment.

1879   The Constitution of the State of California adopted this
        year contained many discriminatory provisions against the
        Chinese, including the prohibition of further immigration
        of Chinese laborers, their removal outside the limits of
        certain cities and towns, and their relocation within pre-
        scribed portions of those limits. It also deprived the Chi-
        nese of employment on any state, county, municipal, or
        other public works. (See Document 4.)

        Congress passed an exclusion law prohibiting further immi-
        gration of Chinese laborers. Since this law contradicted
        the provisions of the Sino-American Treaty of 1868 (Bur-
        lingame Treaty), President Hayes vetoed it.

1880   The League of Deliverance was organized by forty labor
        unions in San Francisco. Under the leadership of Frank
        Roney, the League advised the public to boycott Chinese-
        made goods and to oust the Chinese from their jobs.

        According to a California law enacted this year, any indi-
        vidual or corporation employing any Chinese or Mongolian

was guilty of a misdemeanor and punishable by a fine of not less than $100, nor more than $1,000, or by imprisonment in the county jail of not less than 50 nor more than 500 days, or by both such fine and imprisonment.

November 17. Upon the request of the United States, a Sino-American treaty was signed to revise the Burlingame Treaty. Under the provisions of this new treaty, China agreed to reasonable limitation or suspension, but not absolute prohibition, of the emigration of Chinese laborers to the United States. In return, the American government promised to take measures for the protection of all Chinese already in the United States and to secure to them the same rights and privileges as to nationals of other countries on the most-favored-nation basis. The number of Chinese in the United States then totaled 105,465.

Mobs destroyed all Chinese homes and business properties in Denver, Colorado.

1881

Congress enacted an act to suspend Chinese immigration for twenty years, disregarding the provisions of the Sino-American treaty of 1880. President Arthur considered the act unreasonable and vetoed it.

The convention of the American Federation of Labor, held in Pittsburgh, adopted a resolution urging Congress to prohibit Chinese immigration.

The Chinese government ordered all government-sponsored students in the United States to return to China, largely because of its disappointment with American discriminatory legislation against the Chinese and also the refusal to admit Chinese students to American military and naval academies.

DISCRIMINATORY RESTRICTIONS (1882-1904)

1882

May 6. White workers, particularly those in California, were dissatisfied with the incomplete exclusion of Chinese laborers as stipulated in the 1880 Sino-American treaty, and put strong pressure upon Congress to adopt An Act to Execute Certain Treaty Stipulations Relating to Chinese. Under that act, which was actually in contravention with American treaty obligations, Chinese laborers, unskilled or skilled, were excluded from entering the United States for ten years and the Chinese residing in the United States were not entitled to naturalization. (See Document 5.) The number of Chinese immigrants this year was 39,579, who entered the United States before the enactment of the exclusion law.

August 3. Congress passed the first general immigration law, only a few months after the adoption of the Chinese Exclusion Act.

An examination of mass media in the United States indicated an upswing of anti-Chinese immigration this year. Many liberal business and religious leaders no longer maintained their anti-exclusion stand.

1883   The 1882 Chinese Exclusion Act was chiefly directed at laborers. Chinese of other professions could still come to the United States. While the total number of Chinese immigrants was 8,031 this year, it dropped considerably in the following years.

1884   July 15. Congress passed An Act to Amend An Act Entitled "An Act to Execute Certain Treaty Stipulations Relating to Chinese," Approved May sixth, eighteen hundred and eighty-two. This act imposed more restrictions on the Chinese living in, and their re-entry into, the United States. (See Document 6.)

The Cigar Makers' International Union established Local 224 in San Francisco to force Orientals out of the trade.

The number of Chinese working on farms had increased rapidly in the previous decade,

1885   Due to the severity of a nationwide depression, anti-Chinese agitation reached a stage of savage violence. Some thirty Chinese were killed by white miners in Rock Springs, Wyoming. Delegates from sixty-four Pacific coast labor organizations held an extraordinary congress to discuss a common program against the Chinese.

Fraudulent immigration of Chinese was under Congressional investigation.

November 30. Congress passed an act to prohibit contract labor.

1886   Through various means of threat and violence, white workers in several cities in the states of California (Eureka), Washington (Tacoma and Seattle), and Oregon (Oregon City and Albina) managed to drive out all Chinese residents. Another riot broke out at the mines on Douglas Island in Alaska, where a hundred Chinese were forced to board a small ship and were set adrift at sea. On the other hand, respectable citizens in San Francisco, Seattle, and Oregon City set up organizations to protect the helpless Chinese.

1887   According to the statistics of the Census Bureau, only ten Chinese came to the United States this year.

    October 25. Gim Gong Lue, widely known for his contributions to horticulture (winner of the Wilder Medal), was naturalized as an American citizen in North Adams, Massachusetts.

1888   September 13. The exclusion of Chinese laborers was reaffirmed by another Congressional act. (See Document 7.)

    October 1. Failure to ratify a Sino-American treaty signed on March 12, 1888, by which China was to prohibit Chinese laborers coming to the United States, hastened further legislation by Congress toward that end. It passed An Act to Supplement An Act Entitled "An Act to Execute Certain Treaty Stipulations Relating to Chinese," Approved the sixth day of May, eighteen hundred and eighty-two. Generally known as the Scott Act, it barred the re-entry of Chinese laborers to the United States even if they left the country only temporarily. (See Document 8.) Consequently, over twenty thousand Chinese laborers who left for China with re-entry permits were trapped outside the United States and almost six hundred of them on their way back to the United States were refused permission to land.

1889   In deciding the Chinese Exclusion Case (Chae Chan Ping v. United States), the Supreme Court of the United States ruled that an entire race which the government deemed difficult of assimilation might be barred from entry into the United States and that the exercise of such power should be upheld in the tribunals of the excluding state, regardless of the existence of a prior treaty. (See Document 19.)

    From 1882, when the Chinese Exclusion Act was passed by Congress, to 1889, Chinese population in the United States

had been reduced by 15,360, a loss of almost 2,000 every
year on the average.

1890   The 1890 census reported the number of Chinese in the
            United States as 107,488.

1891   When Henry W. Blair was appointed as American envoy to
            Peking, the Chinese government considered him as persona
            non grata on account of his previous role as a senator in
            passing the Chinese Exclusion Act of 1888. President Har-
            rison interpreted the Chinese position to rest as much on
            the unacceptability of American legislation as on that of
            the person chosen.

            The Chinese in San Francisco published the Chinese World,
            the first bilingual daily in both Chinese and English appearing
            in the United States.

1892   May 5. Congress passed An Act to Prohibit the Coming of
            Chinese Persons into the United States. Known as the
            Geary Act, it extended the Chinese Exclusion Act of 1882
            for another ten years and required certificates of residence
            for Chinese living in the United States. (See Document 9.)

            July 7. The United States Treasury Department issued
            regulations governing applications of Chinese laborers (or
            Chinese persons other than laborers) for certificates of
            residence under the act of May 5, 1892.

1893   After the passing of the Geary Act in 1892, the Chinese
            Community raised a large sum of money to challenge its
            constitutionality before the Supreme Court. In upholding
            the act, the Supreme Court decided, in the case of Fong
            Yue Ting v. United States, that Congress had the right to
            legislate expulsion of Chinese through the order of execu-
            tive officers. (See Document 20.)

            November 3. Congress enacted An Act to Amend An Act
            Entitled "An Act to Prohibit the Coming of Chinese Persons
            into the United States," Approved May fifth, eighteen hun-
            dred and ninety-two. This act made it more difficult for
            Chinese businessmen coming to the United States and im-
            posed additional hardships on those already in the United
            States.

            December 7. Congress passed the Joint Resolution Provid-

ing for the Payment of Salaries and Expense of Additional
Deputy Collectors of Internal Revenue to Carry Out the
Provision of the Chinese Exclusion Act of May 5, 1892, as
Amended by the Act of November 3, 1893.

1894   March 17. The United States and China concluded a treaty
prohibiting the immigration of Chinese laborers for ten
years.

August 18. Congress enacted An Act Making Appropriations for Sundry Civil Expenses of the Government for the
Fiscal Year Ending June 13, 1895, and for Other Purposes.
The immigration officers were authorized to invoke this
act to bar certain aliens, including Chinese, from entering the United States.

Sun Yat-sen, founder of the Chinese Republic, established
his first revolutionary organization, Hsing-chung Hui (Society for the Regeneration of China) in Honolulu, where a
number of Chinese, including his elder brother, joined the
cause.

1895   April 17. The Chinese in the United States were shocked
by the defeat of China by Japan and the conclusion of a hu-
miliating treaty. Many of them became more receptive to
Sun Yat-sen's revolutionary ideas.

A Chinese organization, "The Native Sons of the Golden
State" (later changed to "The Chinese-American Citizens
Alliance" or C.A.C.A.), was founded in San Francisco.
Originally limited to California, its activities gradually
expanded to Chinese communities in other states.

1896   When Li Hung-chang, Prime Minister of the Chinese Imperial Government, visited the United States on his return
journey from Russia, he was greeted by President Cleveland and was invited to many banquets. It is said that
"chop suey" as Chinese food became popular in the United
States around this time. While there are several versions
of its origin and Chinese restaurants have since come into
existence in almost every town of the United States to meet
the demand of American customers, "chop suey" is not a
typical Chinese dish.

In the case of Yick Wo v. Hopkins, United States Supreme
Court found that there was arbitrary administration of

safety ordinances against Chinese laundrymen in San Francisco.

1897   There were 3,363 Chinese coming to the United States, more than any year since 1883.

1898   July 7. Congress passed a joint resolution excluding Chinese laborers from entering Hawaii. (See Document 10.)

The Supreme Court of the United States ruled, in the case of United States v. Wong Kim Ark, that a person born in the United States of Chinese parents is of American nationality by birth. (See Document 21.) Since Wong Kim Ark was born of Chinese parents in 1873, he was also a Chinese national in accordance with Chinese law.

Chee Kung Tong, a politically-oriented Chinese organization in the United States, revitalized its activities.

1899   The United States declared the Open Door Policy toward China, advocating equal treatment within the leased territories and spheres of influence claimed by other powers in China. This policy consequently helped maintain China's territorial integrity and national sovereignty, thus creating tremendous goodwill among the Chinese in both China and the United States toward the American government.

1900   April 29. Congress enacted An Act Making Appropriations for Sundry Civil Expenses of the Government for the Fiscal Year Ending June 13, 1901, and for Other Purposes. This act empowered the immigration commissioner to take charge of the administration of the Chinese Exclusion Law and other related matters.

April 30. Congress passed An Act to Provide a Government for the Territory of Hawaii, under which Chinese in Hawaii were required to apply for certificates of residence.

June 6. Congress passed an act concerning the administration of the Chinese exclusion laws. (See Document 11.)

Chinese treaty merchants and their families enjoyed a special status under United States immigration laws. In United States v. Mrs. Cue Lim, the Supreme Court ruled that the wives and children of Chinese treaty merchants were entitled to come to the United States.

The Boxer Uprising in China against foreign lives and properties was a desperate act of some ignorant Chinese and a
reaction to imperialist aggressions of European powers
and Japan. Their ignominious violence had not only re-
sulted in a heavy indemnity being paid by the Chinese government under the Final Protocol concluded in the following year, but also stirred up anti-Chinese sentiment in the
United States and other countries concerned.

The number of Chinese in the United States totaled 89, 863,
which was 15, 602 less than a decade before. This decrease
indicated that there were more who died and departed than
were born and immigrated.

The Chinese in Honolulu published the New China Daily
News (in Chinese).

1901   March 3. Congress passed An Act Supplementary to An
Act Entitled "An Act to Prohibit the Coming of Chinese Persons into the United States, "Approved May 5, 1892.

1902   March. The foundation of the Dean Lung Chair of Chinese
was inaugurated at Columbia University through the generous contribution of General Horace W. Carpenter. It was
Dean Lung, a domestic of Carpenter, who persuaded his
master to make arrangements with Columbia University
establishing the Chinese department and library. Dean
Lung himself donated all his savings of $12, 000 for that
purpose. This special chair was to commemorate the meri-
torious deed of this humble Chinese immigrant.

April 29. Congress passed An Act to Prohibit the Coming
into and to Regulate the Residence Within the United States,
Its Territories and All Territory under Its Jurisdiction,
and the District of Columbia, of Chinese and Persons of
Chinese Descent. This Act also imposed restrictions upon
the Chinese in the Philippine Islands. (See Document 12.)

A pamphlet entitled "Some Reasons for Chinese Exclusion:
Meat vs. Rice, American Manhood against Asiatic Coolie-
ism--Which Shall Survive?" was published. At the behest
of the Chinese Exclusion Convention of 1901, it was co-au-
thored by Samuel Gompers and Herman Gutstadt, leaders
of the AFL.

In Boston, the police illegally imprisoned and brutally

handled 234 Chinese. Strong protest notwithstanding, none of the officers was censured or punished.

The first Chinese girl student came to the United States.

1903

An American emissary went to China inviting the Chinese merchants to participate in the St. Louis World's Fair. Meanwhile, the Treasury Department laid down discriminatory conditions for admitting Chinese for the exposition.

ABSOLUTE EXCLUSION (1904-1943)

1904

April 27. After the termination of the Sino-American treaty of 1894 prohibiting the immigration of Chinese laborers for ten years, Congress passed another act, extending all Chinese exclusion laws then in existence indefinitely, to be applicable to all insular possessions of the United States.

September 23. The government of the Philippine Islands issued Executive Order 38, extending United States regulations concerning Chinese to the Philippines.

Several Chinese merchants, who responded to the invitation of the United States for the Louisiana Purchase Exposition, were detained and subjected to harsh treatment. The immigration authorities were condemned by the press for their lack of hospitality.

1905

The Asiatic Exclusion League was established by the labor unions in California. Several important leaders responsible for this organization were themselves immigrants-- white immigrants.

In retaliation against American exclusion acts, as well as other abuses and violence suffered by the Chinese in the United States, there started, in China, a nationwide boycott movement against American goods. President Theodore Roosevelt frankly admitted that "we cannot expect China to do us justice," because "the chief cause in bringing about the boycott of our goods in China was undoubtedly our attitude toward the Chinese who came to this country." William H. Taft, then Secretary of War, also publicly criticized the injustice of the Chinese exclusion law and its administration and urged members of Congress and the executive branch to disregard the unreasonable position of the leaders in California who were deeply prejudiced upon the subject.

Sun Yat-sen set up an important revolutionary organization, T'ung-meng Hui (The Alliance), for the overthrow of the Manchu dynasty and the establishment of a republic. Many overseas Chinese, including those in the United States, joined the cause and contributed funds to support its activities.

1906   Because of much criticism against immigration regulations and procedures, the commissioner-general of immigration published the "Compilation of Facts Concerning the Enforcement of the Chinese Exclusion Laws in May, 1906." This report emphasized the specific complaints and difficulty of administration. In pointing out irregular practices of certain desperate Chinese, such as smuggling and illegal entry, it recognized the importance of more decent treatment of the honest ones.

In the opinion of many white workers, the Chinese Exclusion Act of 1882 did not solve the whole problem, because there were about one hundred thousand Chinese laborers already in the United States. Samuel Gompers, a leader of the AFL, thus called for racial purity. This year was also marked by anti-Japanese violence in San Francisco.

Several states, including California, Oregon, and Washington, passed alien land acts, which deprived persons ineligible for citizenship of land holdings.

Fire destroyed the old Chinatown in San Francisco.

1907   February 26. Procedures for interrogation of Chinese entering the United States were provided for in the Regulation Governing the Admission of Chinese. (See Document 13.)

1908   The anti-Chinese pamphlet, "Some Reasons for Chinese Exclusion," was reissued. Meanwhile, Japanese immigration to the United States had become a new menace to white workers.

1909   In its Annual Report, United States Immigration and Naturalization Service frankly admitted that too harsh laws did more harm than good to their enforcement. This statement was particularly true in the case of Chinese exclusion laws.

March 28. The Chinese government promulgated its first
nationality law, regulating the acquisition and loss of Chinese nationality. Voluntary expatriation of Chinese subjects was permitted. Formerly, nationality of the Chinese
was based on the principle of indissoluble natural allegiance and whoever renounced his allegiance would be subject to severe punishment. Under the United States statute
then in force, however, Chinese were ineligible for naturalization.

Yung Wing, the first Chinese student in the United States
and the earliest Chinese to become an American citizen
through naturalization, published his autobiography, My
Life in China and America.

1910
There was a continuing downward trend of the number of
Chinese in the United States in the decade of 1900-1910.
The 1910 census reported only 71,531.

The Young China, another Chinese daily, was published
in San Francisco. This paper has persistently supported
the cause of the Nationalist revolution led by Sun Yat-sen.

1911
March 3. Congress passed another act restricting Chinese
immigration and changing the jurisdiction of Chinese deportation cases.

1912
August 24. Congress passed an act concerning Chinese
immigration and deportation procedures.

November 18. With the inauguration of the Chinese Republic on January 1, 1912, the Chinese nationality law of 1909
was re-enacted.

Yung Wing, the earliest Chinese-American scholar, passed
away in the United States. His American wife, Mary
Louise Kellogg, had died in 1886.

1913
June 23. Congress passed another act concerning the deportation of Chinese under judicial writs.

The China Society of America was formed for the promotion of understandings between the Chinese and Americans.
Among its original sponsors was V. K. Wellington Koo,
formerly Chinese Ambassador to the United States.

1914   December 30. The Chinese nationality law of 1912 was re-
                vised, with no change of voluntary expatriation.

1915   The Immigration and Naturalization Service began to com-
                pile statistics on deportation. Chinese were deported
                largely due to lack of proper documents or staying beyond
                the time limit.

1916   K. C. Li founded the Wah Chang Corporation, which be-
                came the world's largest tungsten refinery by 1953. It
                later expanded into the fields of tin metal, tin alloys, and
                zirconium.

1917   Congress passed another immigration act, providing for
                the barred zones from which natives could not immigrate
                to the United States. It also required reading capacity of
                all aliens over sixteen years of age as one of the conditions
                for admission to the United States.

1918   After China declared war against Germany on August 14,
                1917, thousands of Chinese workers were sent to France.
                Because of their need of assistance in various respects, the
                the International Y.M.C.A. under the leadership of John
                Mott began in this year to recruit a number of Chinese stu-
                dents from different universities in the United States to un-
                dertake the task. Among them were Chih-pao Cheng,
                James Yen, and James Chuan, who later became prominent
                in educational and financial circles in China.

1919   When the Paris Peace Conference of 1919 yielded to Japan's
                claim to former German rights in Shantung against the le-
                gitimate Chinese demand for their restitution to China,
                mass meetings and protest demonstrations were held by
                Chinese students in Peking. Because many of them were
                arrested by the government on May 4, the incident devel-
                oped into a nationwide patriotic movement, with which Chi-
                nese communities and students in the United States ex-
                pressed utmost sympathy. The Chinese delegation even-
                tually refused to sign the Treaty of Versailles by withdraw-
                ing from the conference. The United States Senate was al-
                so extremely dissatisfied with the Treaty of Versailles and
                the arbitrary settlement of the Shantung problem.

1920   There was a further decrease in the number of Chinese in
                the United States in the decade which had just passed, from
                71,531 in 1910 to 61,639 in 1920. However, Chinese females

in this same period markedly increased from 4,675 to 7,748.

1921   May 19. Congress passed the Quota Act, essentially to discourage the immigration of southeastern Europeans to the United States. It eventually led to the enactment of the 1924 act, restricting Chinese and other Asians coming to the United States.

1922   May 26. Congress passed an act to deport violators of narcotics laws. This act applied to immigrants of all nationalities; a few Chinese were deported on that account.

1923   This was the last year that young Chinese in their early formative years could be admitted to the United States under the student status, because the immigration act enacted in the following year laid down specific requirements, such as certificates for admission to American institutions and sufficient funds for education and return to China after graduation.

1924   May 26. Congress passed another immigration act, under which Chinese faced further hardships.

United States Supreme Court decided, in the case of Chang Chan et al. v. John D. Nagle, that Chinese wives of American citizens were not entitled to come to the United States in accordance with the 1924 Immigration Act.

There were 6,992 Chinese immigrants of different professions other than laborers coming to the United States, the highest figure of any single year since 1884.

The Chinese in San Francisco built their own hospitals, "Tung Hwa," because hospital facilities were not always available to them.

1925   According to a decision laid down by the United States Supreme Court this year in the case of Cheuno Sumchee v. Nagle, the 1924 Immigration Act had not affected the status of Chinese treaty merchants or their wives and minor children. The number of Chinese treaty merchants coming to the United States never exceeded 250 per year up to 1943.

From 1892 to 1925, the number of Chinese laborers and other illegal immigrants barred from landing reached 6,327.

1926   The China Institute in America, Inc. was founded under the
              sponsorship of Professor Paul Monroe of Teachers College
              of Columbia University and Pin-wen Kuo, former president
              of the National Southeastern University in Nanking, China.
              Kuo became its first director, succeeded by Chih Meng.
              Much has been done by the Institute toward the promotion
              of Sino-American understanding and of Chinese culture in
              the United States. The present director is Richard Hsu.

1927   The Supreme Court of the United States decided, in Weedin
              v. Chin Bow, that a person born abroad of an American
              parent or parents who had never resided in the United
              States was not of American nationality. Chin Bow was a
              Chinese boy, whose father was an American citizen of Chi-
              nese descent but never resided in the United States. (See
              Document 22,)

1928   After decades of turmoil, China was reunited under the Na-
              tionalist government. While the status of China as a nation
              had been elevated, racial prejudice against Chinese in the
              United States still ran high, as evidenced by the following
              statement of the Stanford University Placement Service on
              the difficulty of placing either a Chinese or Japanese of
              either first or second generation in any kind of position:
              "Many firms have general regulations against employing
              them; others object to them on the grounds that the other
              men employed by the firms do not care to work with them."

              The Supreme Court of the United States decided, in the case
              of Lam Mow v. Nagle, that a child born of Chinese parents
              aboard an American vessel on the high seas was not "born
              in the United States" so as to be deemed a citizen of the
              United States and was thus properly excluded. This deci-
              sion was in apparent conflict with the American traditional
              practice. In Crapo v. Kelly, the same court ruled, in 1872,
              that the territory of Massachusetts itself extended to the
              ship on the high seas.

              The National Dollars Stores, Inc. was founded by the
              Shoong family. Originally started as a small store in San
              Francisco in 1907, it had developed into a chain with over
              fifty branches in California, Washington, Utah, Arizona,
              and Hawaii by this year. Joseph Shoong, the guiding spirit
              of the company, became one of the wealthiest Chinese-
              Americans. A generous philanthropist, he contributed
              much of his wealth to worthy individuals and institutions.

1929   February 5. The National Government in Nanking promul-
                gated a new nationality law which stipulated procedures for
                acquisition and loss of Chinese nationality in detail. Ar-
                ticle 11 reads: "One who wishes to acquire the nationality
                of a foreign country may be permitted by the Ministry of
                the Interior to renounce his (or her) Chinese nationality
                provided that he (or she) is more than twenty years of age
                and has legal capacity under the Chinese law." According
                to that law, voluntary expatriation by a man does not extend
                to his wife and children. It is also important to note that
                if a Chinese national becomes an American citizen through
                naturalization without obtaining prior permission of the
                Chinese government to renounce his Chinese citizenship,
                he will most likely possess dual nationality.

                Another Chinese fraternal organization, the Sam King As-
                sociation, was established this year, representing the Chi-
                nese coming from the eastern provinces of China, includ-
                ing Kiangsu, Chekiang, and Kiangsi. Its membership has
                increased rapidly since 1949, because more Chinese from
                that region immigrated to the United States after the change
                of power on the mainland.

1930   There was a slight increase of the number of Chinese in the
                United States in the previous decade, totaling 74,954. The
                number of Chinese females almost doubled during the same
                period, reaching 15,152.

1931   September 18. Japan invaded Manchuria. Overseas Chi-
                nese, including those in the United States, were indignant
                at the unprovoked aggression and contributed heavilty to
                the Chinese government for national defense.

                The last of the so-called tong wars occurred this year.
                Tong, meaning "hall," represented different fraternal or-
                ganizations of the Chinese in the United States. As time
                went by, some conflict of interests developed among them.
                Although the infamous tong wars belonged to past history,
                they had somewhat tarnished the law-abiding and peace-
                loving reputation of the Chinese in this country.

1932   The United States government was much conerned with Ja-
                pan's military occupation of Manchuria. On January 7, 1932,
                Secretary Henry L. Stimson declared the doctrine of non-
                recognition of any situation created by forcible means.
                Completely ignoring the American protest, Japan invaded

Shanghai on January 28, and set up the puppet state "Man-chukuo" on February 18. The Chinese in the United States fully supported the American policy and continued to render financial assistance to the Chinese government.

1933   A well-known study on American preferred ethnic groups made public this year listed Canadians, English, Scots, Irish, French, Swedes, Germans, and Spaniards. The reasons for the low-ranking of the Chinese were many, including differences of races, social traditions, and historical backgrounds. Findings in later years reached similar conclusions. It has, however, been generally recognized that the Chinese in the United States have a low percentage of juvenile delinquency due to close family bonds and disciplined education.

1934   A decade after the passing of the 1924 Immigration Act, there came to the United States less than one hundred Chinese teachers and ministers, as well as their wives and children, even though they were entitled to preferential treatment under the law.

1935   Lin Yutang published his well-known work, My Country and My People. Followed by several others, this book helped Americans understand China and the Chinese.

1936   December 12-25. All the papers in the United States, particularly the Chinese dailies, printed headlines about the Sian incident, when Chiang Kai-shek was forcibly detained by his two generals, Chang Hsueh-liang and Yang Hu-cheng on December 12. Concerned with Chiang's personal danger at a time when his leadership was much needed against Japan's further intrusion in North China, many Chinese organizations in this country sent cables back to the rebels, urging their release of Chiang, who was shortly set free on December 25.

1937   July 7. The full-scale war between China and Japan broke out at Lukou-ch'iao (Marco Polo Bridge). The government and people of the United States were shocked at this new crisis. Chinese communities in various American cities reinforced their efforts to make financial contributions to the Chinese government against aggression.

Lin Yutang, author of My Country and My People, published his best seller, The Importance of Living. Both of these works have promoted American interest in the life and philosophy of the Chinese.

1938   Hiram Fong, a distinguished citizen of Hawaii, was elected to the legislature of the Territory of Hawaii.

1939   Yuan-ren Chao, a prominent Chinese scholar of linguistics, came to teach at Yale University from the University of Hawaii. He later taught at the University of California from 1952 until his retirement in 1960. Author of many works, Chao has been widely known for his contributions to this special field.

1940   The decade of 1930-1940 revealed a decrease of Chinese males and a rapid increase of females in the United States. Of the total number of 77,504 in 1940, there were 57,389 males and 20,115 females.

There were twenty-eight cities in the United States having Chinatowns, which were decreasing as time passed by. Some old Chinatowns, founded by miners and railroad laborers in early days, disappeared when they moved out. Through gradual integration and slum clearing, still others were merged with other areas.

Among many Chinese artists in the United States, Kingman Dong is comparatively better known. His paintings won international recognition and were displayed in most of the major museums. While his works were exhibited as early as the 1930's, the Metropolitan Museum of Art acquired its first Dong painting in 1940.

1941   Chinese newspapers in the United States unanimously praised the Atlantic Charter declared by President Franklin D. Roosevelt and Prime Minister Winston Churchill on August 14, 1941. They considered it a definite step of the American government moving toward collective sanctions against the aggressors.

1942   Lack of transportation facilities after American entry into World War II had restricted the traveling of ordinary civilians to the United States to the minimum. Thus, up to the year before Allied victory over Japan, only twenty-four Chinese were debarred from landing.

GRADUAL LIBERALIZATION (1943--)

1943

January 11. A new treaty was signed between the United States and China, entitled "Treaty for the Relinquishment of Extraterritorial Rights in China and the Regulation of Related Matters." It abolished all unilateral rights and privileges previously acquired by the United States in China, and opened up a new epoch of Sino-American relations. (See Document 17.) This treaty led to the eventual repeal of all Chinese exclusion laws by the United States before the end of the year.

December 17. Congress passed An Act to Repeal the Chinese Exclusion Acts, to Establish Quotas, and for Other Purposes. (See Document 14.) The elimination of discriminatory legislation against Chinese immigration had also raised the status of the Chinese already in the United States. Actually, the Chinese were not treated on the same basis as the Europeans, because this act established a quota of only 105 for Chinese every year. This figure was one-sixth of one percent of the number of the Chinese in the United States in 1920 as determined by the census of that year. Besides, the final authority of selection among the applicants was vested in the United States government.

There were 78,000 Chinese in the United States this year. When the Chinese exclusion acts were fully enforced, the number of departed Chinese was 37,738 more than the immigrants during the period 1908-1943. Among the factors contributing to this decrease were legal restrictions, racial prejudice, economic depression, and scarcity of Chinese females.

The Yale Institute of Far Eastern Languages was founded, focusing on teaching Chinese language and culture.

1944

K. C. Li, one of the most successful Chinese industrialists in the United States, established the Li Foundation, providing fellowships to students working for advanced degrees.

Ko-kwei Chen, research director of the Eli Lilly Company since 1929, was awarded the Certificate of Merit by the American Medical Association.

1945

In spite of the repeal of the Chinese exclusion acts, Chinese quota immigrants to the United States in the ensuing

decade were generally below one hundred as selected by
the American government. There were, however, non-
quota immigrants at the same time; more Chinese scholars
came to teach in the United States, on an average of about
137 each year in comparison with 10 per year during the
previous decade.

The Hung Man Ming Chi party was established as a result
of the reorganization of the Chee Kung Tong, a politically
influential organization of the Chinese community in the
United States.

1946   Subsequent to the War Bride Act of December 28, 1945, Congress passed a bill enabling wives and children of Chinese-
American citizens to apply as non-quota immigrants.

Chih Tsang, a close associate of K. P. Ch'en, a successful financier in China, and secretary-general of the Universal Trading Corporation from 1942 to 1945, founded the China Trade & Industrial Service, Inc. It exported machinery
and other goods to China in the postwar period to meet the
need for her recovery and reconstruction.

Wing F. Ong was elected to the Arizona state legislature.
He was the first American of Chinese descent to sit in a
state legislature in the United States.

By the end of 1946, there were fourteen Chinese dailies out
of ninety-five foreign language newspapers in the United
States.

1947   Partly due to the worsening situation in postwar China, the
number of Chinese immigrants to the United States drastic-
ally increased this year. The total number was 1,128, most
of whom came on non-quota basis.

Remittances from overseas Chinese had long helped the
Chinese government to offset China's unfavorable trade
balance. The amount sent by the Chinese in the United
States during the period of China's full-scale war with Japan and two postwar years (1938-1947) reached seventy million dollars, largely to their families and relatives in China, but a certain portion representing their contributions
to the Chinese government for worthy causes.

Eddie Gong, a grandson of a Chinese immigrant in laundry

business, was named "Boy President of the U.S.A.," and was warmly received by President Harry S. Truman at an American Legion ceremony in Washington, D.C. He was then a high school student, and later graduated from Harvard University.

1948   June 25. The Displaced Persons Act provided some relief to the Chinese already in the United States, who were able to change their status under stipulated conditions. This act was later amended, and eventually expired on June 30, 1954.

Elected to the legislature of Hawaii in 1938, Hiram Fong was elevated to the position of Speaker of the House.

Wing F. Ong was re-elected to the Arizona state legislature.

1949   This year marked the Communist conquest of China's mainland. There were 2,490 Chinese coming to the United States. Because of the domestic development in China, many Chinese students remained in this country even after completion of their studies. According to "A Survey of Chinese Students in American Universities and Colleges in the Past One Hundred Years," prepared by the National Tsing Hua University Research Fellowship Fund and China Institute in America (published in New York, 1954), the total number of these students reached 3,914 in the academic year 1948-1949, an all-time high.

1950   June 16. The second Displaced Persons Act gave Chinese in the United States further relief for adjustment of their status.

According to the 1950 census, the total number of Chinese in the United States, including Hawaii, reached 150,005.

Prejudices against Chinese were still not uncommon. Betty Lee Sung, author of Mountain of Gold, found an example of flagrant discrimination in a government agency. The division chief of that agency frankly told her that he wanted an American-American not a Chinese-American to head its section dealing with Far Eastern affairs. The man evidently did not realize that only the Indians are American-Americans and all other Americans of different ethnic origins came from other parts of the world.

Jade Snow Wong's Fifth Chinese Daughter was published.
It was a fascinating and perceptive memoir written by a
young Chinese-American, who vividly described her early
life and family traditions in San Francisco.

1951   The United States Foreign Assets Control Board prohibited
remittances to mainland China subsequent to the People's
Republic's entrance into the Korean War. Many Chinese
in the United States still had families in China, who were
thus deprived of financial assistance as a result of that
order.

Violinist Si-hon Ma, husband of pianist Kwong-kwong Tung,
was a recipient of the Heifetz Award at Tanglewood.

1952   The Sino-American Amity, a non-political organization,
was founded in New York by Paul Cardinal Yu Pin. To foster a better understanding and a closer friendly relationship between the Chinese and American peoples, it has of-
fered educational, cultural, and social programs of wide
scope.

Mrs. Toy Len Goon of Maine was chosen America's "Mother of the Year." Mrs. Truman conferred this title upon
her in Washington, D.C. After the death of her husband in
1940, she raised her eight children by operating a small
laundry. They all received higher education and pursued
successful careers in different professions.

December 24. When the Immigration and Nationality Law,
known as the McCarran-Walter Act, came into effect, it
removed the inequality against Chinese women, who were
previously not entitled to the same privileges under non-
quota status as Chinese men. Like the 1924 act, it still
upheld the national-origin quota, which, in effect, was discriminatory against the Chinese and other peoples from
the Asia-Pacific area. From the enactment of the 1952 act
up to the end of 1960, however, 27,502 Chinese immigrants
were admitted to the United States.

1953   The Refugee Relief Act of 1953, which was later amended
and expired at the end of 1956, apportioned 2,000 for Chinese out of a total of 205,000 non-quota immigrants.

August. The Air Force announced a new electronic tube
producing radar power of four million watts, which was de-

veloped by Dr. Chao-chen Wang of the Sperry Gyroscope
Company and his associate, Dr. C. E. Rich.

1954

There were 2,747 Chinese who arrived in the United States
this year, more than twice the number of any other year
from 1950 to 1953. Many of them came as refugees. This
upward trend continued for a while with slight variations.
The ratio between Chinese males and females in this country became more balanced.

August 5. Because of the participation of the People's Republic in the Korean War, the United States government issued a restraining order under which Chinese scholars with
technical knowledge which might be beneficial to an enemy
country were not permitted to leave the United States. A
group of twenty-six Chinese students petitioned to the President of the United States, urging him to revoke that order.

September 21. The New York Times printed a full-page
advertisement by seventy-seven Chinese organizations in
the United States, plus one in Cuba, opposing the seating
of the People's Republic of China in the United Nations.
The most important ones were sixteen Chinese Consolidated
Benevolent Associations (Chung Hwa Kung So or the Chinese
Societies) in San Francisco and several major cities with
large Chinese population. The other sixty-one were all in
New York.

According to a survey made by the China Institute in America, there were sixty-four Chinese scholars teaching Chinese history, culture, and language at different American
universities and colleges.

Upon the request of the State Department, Kingman Dong
represented the United States as a special cultural envoy
to the Orient and later other parts of the world. He had
won tremendous goodwill for the country by his speeches
and exhibition of his paintings.

November 1. Under a sensational headline, "China Mathe-
matician Solves Firm's Dilemma," The Philadelphia In-
quirer reported how Dr. Peter Pei-chi Chow solved the vi-
bration problem of a very special type of loom for the Bear-
ing Products Company of Philadelphia.

The United Board for Christian Colleges in China, with headquarters in New York, has long been responsible for promoting Chinese higher education. Dr. Theodore Hsi-en Chen, head of the department of Asian studies of the University of Southern California, was sent to Taiwan as its representative to help establish the Tunghai University on the island.

1955   According to a survey made by Dr. Peter Sih, only sixteen cities in the United States had Chinatowns, a decrease of twelve in fifteen years.

The United Council of Christian Churches made a survey of churches in the United States which were essentially of Chinese membership. According to its report, there were sixty-six Protestant churches, including four in Hawaii. It should also be noted that, in recent years, several Buddhist temples were founded.

An Wang, a specialist in electronic calculators, founded the Wang Laboratories. It manufactures a broad line of electronic programmable desk calculators and associated peripheral equipment for business, scientific, and engineering applications.

Kuan H. Sun, a noted writer on physics and holder of approximately fifty patents, became the manager of the Westinghouse radiation and nucleonics laboratory.

James Wong Howe has long been the highest paid cameraman in Hollywood. He worked for MGM, Columbia Pictures, Fox Studios, Warner Brothers, and other major motion picture companies. For the superb effects in filming "The Rose Tattoo," he won another Oscar for cinematography.

Seventy-six Chinese intellectuals left the United States for mainland China. Some of them went for ideological reasons; others, to seek family reunions.

1956   While racial prejudices were still in existence, some business firms were more enlightened than others according to a survey in 1956. IBM in Poughkeepsie, New York, for instance, employed many Chinese professionals, some of them were even in supervisory positions.

Chih Tsang, founder of China Trade & Industrial Service,

Inc., established the New World Research Corporation, which has been conducting business with some forty countries. Tsang has been known in the business world for his absolute devotion and integrity.

December 1. The Refugee Relief Act of 1953 expired.

1957

The Nobel Prize for physics was conferred on two scientists of Chinese descent, Chen-ning Yang and Tsung-dao Lee, a member of the Institute for Advanced Study at Princeton and Professor of Physics at Columbia University respectively. They jointly discovered a new order of universe that shattered the "Principle of the Conservation of Parity."

March 5-7. A nationwide conference of representatives from different Chinese organizations in the United States, including thirty-four Chinese Consolidated Benevolent Associations, was held in Washington, D.C. It issued a declaration, emphasizing close cooperation of all Chinese-Americans and full support of the United States policy toward China.

According to a survey made by the Advisory Committee on Cultural Relations in America, there were 219 educational institutions in the United States offering some courses on China, and only 127 students majoring in Chinese studies.

September 11. Over two thousand Chinese were benefited by the Refugee Escapee Act, which extended the unused allotments of the 1953 Act.

C. Y. Lee published his first novel, The Flower Drum Song, in which he described the life of the Chinatown in San Francisco.

1958

The American Association of Teachers of Chinese Language and Culture (AATCLC) was established under the sponsorship of Chi-pao Cheng, who became its first executive secretary. It has now a membership of over four hundred scholars from different universities and colleges in the United States. Cheng was later succeeded by Dr. Paul K. T. Sih, director of the Center of Asian Studies, St. John's University, New York.

As described before, Chen-ning Yang and Tsung-dao Lee had discovered a new order of universe and won the Nobel

Physics Prize in the preceding year. It was Dr. Chien-shiung Wu, professor of physics at Columbia University who conducted their experiments. In recognition of her important contributions to experimental physics, Princeton University conferred on her an honorary doctorate in science, its first one to a woman.

1959   January 23. Delbert E. Wong was appointed by Governor Edmund G. Brown to a municipal bench in Los Angeles. He was the first Chinese-American to become a judge.

July. In Hawaii, Hiram L. Fong, speaker of the house of the state legislature, was elected United States senator. A Republican, Fong was the first senator from Hawaii, where the Democrats have held predominant influence.

September 22. Congress passed an act under which more Chinese on the quota waiting list obtained non-quota status.

The number of Chinese coming to the United States reached 6,031 this year.

1960   The number of Chinese in the United States as reported by the 1960 census reached 237,292 (135,549 male, 101,743 female; about 60% native born). Their occupations were quite diversified as shown by the following percentages: professional, technical, and kindred workers, 16.8%; managers, officials, and proprietors, 5.4%; clerical and kindred workers, 30.1%; farmers and farm managers, 0.3%; crafts, foremen, and kindred workers, 0.8%; sales workers, 8%; other workers, including operatives, household, service, and laborers, 32.1%; unreported, 6.3%. More than one-half of the Chinese lived in four cities: Honolulu, San Francisco, Oakland, and New York.

From 1943, when all Chinese exclusion acts were repealed, to this year, 22,329 Chinese had become American citizens through naturalization. Most of them changed allegiance after the Chinese Communists took over the mainland.

By the end of this year, Chinese newspapers had been reduced to eleven out of sixty-five foreign language dailies.

C. C. Li, professor of biometry and director of the Human Genetics Training Program at the University of Pittsburgh, was elected president of the American Society of Human

Genetics.

Several honors were conferred upon Chinese scholars this year. Among them was Dr. Kung-chuan Hsiao, professor of Far Eastern studies at the University of Washington. In awarding him a special prize of $10,000, the American Council of Learned Societies cited: "Professor K. C. Hsiao combines the best of two great scholarly traditions, those of China and the West."

James Wong Howe was complimented by <u>Newsweek</u> (January 11) as the finest movie cameraman in the world.

Wing Wu ran for the House of Representatives of Rhode Island. As a Republican candidate in a year of Democratic sweep, he lost the election.

1961

The total number of Chinese admitted to the United States from 1899 to 1961 was 110,480, according to a report released by the Immigration and Naturalization Service in February 1964. This was a very small figure in comparison with the number of European immigrants during the same period.

The Office of Cultural Attaché of the Chinese Embassy in Washington, D.C. reported that there were more than thirteen hundred Chinese on the faculties of eighty-eight American universities and colleges, some of whom held administrative positions, such as deans and departmental chairmen. The number constantly increased in the following decade.

1962

To relieve the refugee situation in Hongkong, President John F. Kennedy permitted the entry into the United States of several thousand Chinese as parolees. Their total number eventually reached over fifteen thousand by the end of 1965.

At age thirty-six, Wing Luke was elected to the Seattle City Council and became president <u>pro tempore</u>.

A distinguished biochemist, Dr. Choh-hao Li won the Albert Lasker Medical Research Award, which was conferred on him by Mrs. Lyndon Johnson with an honorarium of $10,000.

1963

In his special message to Congress on immigration, President John F. Kennedy emphasized that "it is time to correct the mistakes of the past and work toward a better future for all humanity."

Ju Chin Chu, professor of chemical engineering at the Polytechnic Institute of Brooklyn, represented the United States at the NATO Conference on Propulsion. Well known in his field, Chu has served as consultant of many government agencies and corporations in the United States.

1964   During the period 1944-1964, over thirty-seven thousand Chinese in the United States completed their naturalization process to become American citizens.

Ieoh Ming Pei, one of the best architects in the West, was chosen by the Kennedy family above a selected group of internationally known architects to design the John F. Kennedy Memorial Library.

November. Hiram L. Fong was re-elected to the United States Senate with an overwhelming majority against the Democratic landslide of President Lyndon B. Johnson.

1965   The annual number of Chinese quota immigrants from 1954 to 1965 exceeded the apportioned figure except during 1962-1964. The increase was attributed to the adjusted status of many Chinese as displaced persons and also as a result of suspension of deportation by private bills.

October 3. Congress passed a new and more liberal immigration and nationality act. It made sweeping changes by abolishing national-origin quotas and establishing, on principle, a first-come-first-served basis. Country of origin was no longer based on nationality or race but on place of birth. Instead of a quota of 105, Chinese could possibly use up to 20,000 of the annual quota.

Edward Hong, a Republican, was defeated in his campaign for New York state assemblyman.

1966   After the liberalization of Chinese immigration consequent to the enactment of the 1965 act, there was a steady increase of Chinese immigrants to the United States, and many temporary visitors had readjusted their status to permanent residents. Up to the end of June of this year, the number of new arrivals totaled 17,508 (including 3,872 from Hongkong), and 9,770 Chinese already in the United States on temporary basis obtained the status of permanent residents.

Benefited by federal grants for Chinese studies provided by the National Defense Educational Act, over 60 American institutions began to offer degree programs in Chinese studies, with about 2,500 students. By the end of 1966, there were approximately 1,450 Chinese scholars of different specializations on the instructional staffs of different American universities and colleges. Most of them came to the United States in the last two decades.

A distinguished citizen of Oxnard, California, William D. Soo Hoo was elected mayor of that city, which had only sixty ethnic Chinese among a population of sixty-four thousand.

Gerald Tsai, Jr. surprised Wall Street in February, when he easily amassed $270 million of capital from 150,000 investors to found the Manhattan Fund, of which he became the president. He was born in Shanghai, and naturalized as an American citizen in 1957.

In its December 26 issue, U.S. News and World Report wrote: "Visit 'Chinatown U.S.A.' and you find an important racial minority pulling itself up from hardship and discrimination to become a model of self-respect and achievement in today's America." Complimenting the Chinese low rate of crime, it went further to state that "in crime-ridden cities, Chinese districts turn up as islands of peace and stability."

1967

Up to June 30, there were 25,096 Chinese coming to the United States this year, and as many as 11,069 Chinese already in the United States on temporary basis readjusted their status to permanent residents.

President Lyndon B. Johnson appointed the Kerner Commission to inquire into the causes of civil disorders. The report pointed out that white society was deeply implicated in the ghetto. Although the investigation was chiefly directed into the situation of the blacks, its conclusions can be equally applied to that of the Chinese and other minorities.

1968

By the end of June, there were 16,434 Chinese coming to

the United States, and 4,927 Chinese already in the United States changed their status from temporary basis to permanent residents.

Dr. William L. Tung published International Law in an Organizing World, which discussed, among many other subjects, state responsibility for the protection of resident aliens and national minorities.

1969   Up to June 30, there were 20,893 Chinese coming to the United States. Among those Chinese already in the United States on a temporary basis, 3,980 were able to adjust their status to permanent residents.

December 5. The immigration and nationality act of 1965 was amended, requiring a waiting period of thirty days for the issuance of any certificate of naturalization after the filing of the petition for naturalization, unless the attorney general decides to waive such a period in certain cases. This requirement applied to all aliens, including the Chinese.

1970   February. A bilingual paper, Getting Together, was issued by I Wor Kuen in New York. This new organization, set up by a group of young Chinese in the preceding year, began to challenge the authority of older establishments in Chinatown.

The Immigration and Nationality Act of 1965 was amended twice this year (April 7, July 10), concerning procedures for admitting aliens with special ability and those coming to the United States under government financed programs, as well as the conditions for depositing bonds. These provisions applied to all aliens, including the Chinese.

There were 17,956 Chinese coming to the United States by the end of June, and 5,899 Chinese already in the United States established their status as permanent residents.

The 1970 census revealed the total number of Chinese in the United States as 435,062, which indicated an increase of 83,32% from the figure of the 1960 census. They were no longer concentrated on the west coast, even though California still had the highest number of 170,131. Next to California were New York State (81,378), Hawaii (52,039), Illinois (14,474), Massachusetts (14,012), Washington (9,201),

New Jersey (9,233), Texas (7,635), Pennsylvania (7,053),
Maryland (6,520), Michigan (6,407), and Ohio (5,305).
Thus their geographical distribution was much wider than
before, expanding gradually from the west to other regions.
According to the same census, Chinese constituted only
one-fifth of one percent of the 1970 population in the United
States, one of the smallest minorities. While the rate of
intermarriage was up 63% in the last decade, the percentage of Chinese men married to white wives was 8.3%.

November. Senator Hiram Fong of Hawaii was re-elected
for a third term.

1971

There were 17,622 Chinese coming to the United States by
the end of June of this year, and 6,747 Chinese already in
the United States changed their status from temporary basis
to permanent residents. From the effective date of the
1965 immigration and nationality act to the middle of 1971,
there were as many as 115,509 Chinese coming to the United
States, with almost equal distribution between males and females. During the same period, 42,392 Chinese already
in the United States on temporary basis were able to read-
just their status to permanent residents with the intention
to become American citizens through naturalization.

Foreign students in American universities and colleges,
steadily increased in the previous sixteen years. For the
academic year 1970-1971, the total number was 144,708.
Those from Asia occupied 37%, the highest percentage in
comparison with other areas. Ethnic Chinese totaled
21,355 from the following places: Taiwan (9,210); Hongkong
(9,040); Singapore, Malaysia, Thailand, and the Philippines
(3,105). Next in order were Canadians (12,595) and Indians
(12,523). In many parts of the world, ethnic Chinese established their own educational institutions to teach their
children Chinese language and culture. By the end of June,
1971, their number reached 4,372 (higher education, 34;
high schools, 245; junior high schools, 325; vocational
schools, 24; elementary schools and kindergartens, 3,744).
Among these, 97.45% were in Asia, and only 1.48% in
America. This big difference of percentage was due to the
concentration of Chinese in Southeast Asia. Many ethnic
Chinese have also gone to China for advanced studies.

Beginning in the latter part of this year, scores of Chinese-
Americans visited the mainland, including Dr. Chen-ning

Yang (professor of physics at the State University of New
York at Stony Brook), Dr. Chun-tu Hsueh (professor of political science at University of Maryland), Way Dong Woo
(a Boston industrialist), and Tommy Lee (a businessman in
New York City).

1972   The visit of President Richard M. Nixon to Peking on February 21 marked a new era of Sino-American relations, and
also created a sensation among the Chinese in the United
States. This was climaxed by the joint communique by
President Nixon and Premier Chou En-lai of the People's
Republic of China in Shanghai on February 25. Many Chinese in the United States, particularly businessmen who
were sentimentally inclined to the Republic of China in Taiwan, had, however, expressed dismay at the sudden change
of American policy.

There was a steady increase of visitors between China and
the United States this year. The State Department estimated about fifteen hundred to two thousand Americans
going to the mainland. Many of them were scholars of Chinese descent, including the Nobel laureates Chen-ming
Yang and Tsung-dao Lee.

The University of Pennsylvania conferred an honorary degree of doctor of laws upon Dr. Yu-hsiu Ku, professor of
electrical engineering (1952-1972) in recognition of his out-
standing contributions to analysis of the transit behavior of
a-c machines and systems. A renowned educator in China,
Ku came to the United States in 1950, first teaching at
M.I.T. before moving to Pennsylvania. Author of several
books in his field as well as Chinese poems and songs, Ku
has also been active in a number of cultural organizations
sponsored by the Chinese in the United States.

October 27. The immigration and nationality act of 1965
was further amended, whereby a naturalized American citizen is required to comply with either of the following conditions in order to keep his nationality: (1) he comes to the
United States and continues to stay for a period of no less
than two years between the ages of fourteen years and twenty-
eight years; or (2) the alien parent is naturalized while the
child is under the age of eighteen years and the child begins
to reside permanently in the United States while under the
age of eighteen years (temporary absence from the United
States of less than sixty days not considered as breaking

the continuity of his physical presence). This provision applies to people of all ethnic origins, including those of Chinese descent.

In spite of the generally downward demand for foreign-language dailies in the United States, the number of Chinese newspapers in New York City increased to six, resulting in too much competition and limited circulation. These are: The Chinese Journal, The United Journal, The China Tribune, The China Times, Sing Tao Jih Pao, and The China Post. The last one came into existence in 1972. In addition, there are four more Chinese dailies in San Francisco (The Young China and Chinese Times) and Honolulu (United Chinese Press and New Chinese Daily News). The Chinese in several major cities have also published a number of weeklies, monthlies, and other periodicals.

1973

February 3. This was the Chinese New Year's Day of the Year of Ox according to the Chinese traditional calendar. Both President Richard Nixon and Vice-President Spiro Agnew sent congratulatory messages to many Chinese-Americans.

Mrs. Anna Chennault, widow of General Claire Lee Chennault, was named to a three-year term on the Women's Advisory Committee of the Federal Aviation Administration. Mrs. Chennault has long been active in Republican politics, and is currently vice-president for international affairs of the Flying Tiger Line, an all cargo airline.

Gerald Tsai, Jr. resigned as president and chief executive of the Tsai Management & Research Corporation and its five mutual funds, including the Manhattan Fund. Perhaps the best-known mutual fund executive during the era of the go-go funds in the late 1960's, Tsai was negotiating to acquire controlling interests in a New York Stock Exchange brokerage house.

June 9. The Organization of Chinese-Americans (OCA) was established in the District of Columbia. A non-partisan coalition of many Chinese-Americans, it is designed to help solve various problems confronting the Chinese who have become either American citizens or permanent residents of the United States.

September 1-3. At the annual convention for Chinese students, alumni, and their friends, sponsored by the China Institute in America, a special panel was arranged to examine the social and personal problems of Chinese in America. Among the participants were Mr. David Fung (Instructor of Chinese Language at the China Institute), Dr. Richard P. Wang (Staff Psychiatrist of New Jersey Neuro-psychiatric Institute), and Dr. William L. Tung (Professor of Political Science, Queens College of The City University of New York). Several important topics were discussed, including discrimination, assimilation, and diversified interests among Chinese-Americans.

September 8. Over one thousand Americans and Chinese attended the dedication ceremony of the Sun Yat Sen Memorial Hall at St. John's University, New York. The construction of this unique building of Oriental architecture, named in honor of the founder of the Chinese republic, was made possible through generous contributions of many Americans and Chinese in the United States and abroad. The hall now houses the Center of Asian Studies, which is under the directorship of Dr. Paul K. T. Sih, professor of history and assistant to the president of the university.

PART II

DOCUMENTS

PART II.   DOCUMENTS

The twenty-two documents embodied in this book do not represent a comprehensive collection relating to Chinese immigration to the United States, but are a selection of a few notable ones for illustration. They are divided into three sections:

A.   Federal and state laws, including those enacted by the state legislature of California where the Chinese immigrants first settled;

B.   Treaties between the United States and China, containing the texts of the first treaty of Wanghia of 1844, the Burlingame Treaty of 1868 providing for free and voluntary emigration, and the treaty of 1943 for the relinquishment of extraterritoriality and other unilateral rights and privileges of the United States in China; and

C.   Judicial decisions concerning the immigration and status of the Chinese, four by the Supreme Court of the United States and one by the Supreme Court of the State of California.

All these documents are numbered in chronological order under each category and have been briefly described in Part I(Chronology) for the convenience of cross reference.

A.   FEDERAL AND STATE LAWS

Document 1

AN ACT TO DISCOURAGE THE IMMIGRATION TO THIS STATE OF PERSONS WHO CANNOT BECOME CITIZENS THEREOF
April 28, 1855

The People of the State of California, represented in Senate and Assembly, do enact as follows:

SECTION 1.   The master, owner, or consignee of any vessel, arriving in any of the ports of this State from any foreign State, country, or territory, having on board any persons who are incompetent by the laws of the United States or the laws and constitution of this State to become citizens thereof are hereby required to pay a tax, for each such person, of fifty dollars.

SECTION 2.   It shall be the duty of the Commissioner of Emigrants of the City of San Francisco, or the Mayor or other chief municipal officer of any town or city in other parts of this State, to visit all such vessels immediately upon their arrival in any of said ports, and whenever the said Commissioner, Mayor, or other chief municipal officer shall be satisfied by personal inspection, or otherwise, of the number of passengers referred to in the first section of this Act, on board of said vessel, he shall demand and receive of the master, owner, or consignee of such vessel, the sum of fifty dollars for each such passenger so disqualified from becoming a citizen of the United States.

SECTION 3.   In the event of the nonpayment of said tax within three days after the arrival of said vessel, or within three days after demand for said tax, said Commissioner, Mayor, or chief officer of any city, town, or village, shall commence suit in the name of the State against the master, owner, or consignee, or all of them for said tax before any court of competent jurisdiction in said town or city; and the commencing of said suit shall constitute a lien upon such vessel for the amount of said tax, and it shall be forever liable for the same.

SECTION 4.   The Commissioner of Emigrants of San Francisco is hereby required to pay over on the first Monday of every month to the Treasurer of State, for the use of the Hospital Fund, all moneys collected under the provisions of this Act, reserving to himself first five percent of the amount so collected as compensation under this Act.

SECTION 5.   The said Commissioner of Emigrants is required, before entering upon the duties of this Act, to enter into a bond to the State of California in the sum of thirty thousand dollars, with good and sufficient security to be approved by the Governor, conditioned that he will well and truly discharge all the duties required of him by this Act, which said bond shall be filed in the office of the Secretary of State.

SECTION 6. This Act shall take effect from and after the first day of September next.

Document 2

AN ACT TO PREVENT THE FURTHER IMMIGRATION OF CHINESE
OR MONGOLIANS TO THIS STATE [CALIFORNIA]
April 26, 1858

SECTION 1. On and after the first day of October, anno Domini, eighteen hundred and eighty-five, any person, or persons, of the Chinese or Mongolian races, shall not be permitted to enter this State, or land therein, at any port or part thereof, and it shall be unlawful for any man, or persons, whether captain or commander, or other person, in charge of, or interested in, or employed on board of, or passengers upon, any vessel or vessels of any nature or description whatsoever, to knowingly allow, or permit, any Chinese or Mongolian, on and after such time, to enter any of the ports of this State, to land therein, or at any place or places, within the border of this State, and any person or persons violating any of the provisions of this Act, shall be held and deemed guilty of a misdemeanor, and upon conviction thereof shall be subject to a fine in any sum not less than four hundred dollars, nor more than six hundred dollars, for each and every offense, or imprisonment in the County Jail of the County in which the said offense was committed, for a period of not less than three months, nor more than one year, or by both such fine and imprisionment.

SECTION 2. The landing of each and every Chinese or Mongolian person, or persons, shall be deemed and held as a distinct and separate offense, and punished accordingly.

Document 3

AN ACT TO PROTECT FREE WHITE LABOR AGAINST COMPETITION WITH CHINESE COOLIE LABOR, AND TO DISCOURAGE THE IMMIGRATION OF THE CHINESE INTO THE STATE OF CALIFORNIA
April 26, 1862

The People of the State of California, represented in Senate and Assembly, do enact as follows:

SECTION 1. There is hereby levied on each person, male and female, of the Mongolian race, of the age of eighteen years and upwards, residing in this State, except such as shall, under laws now existing, or which may hereafter be enacted, take out licenses to work in the mines, or to prosecute some kind of business, a monthly capitation tax of two dollars and fifty cents, which tax shall be known as the Chinese Police Tax; provided, That all Mongolians exclusively engaged in the production and manufacture of the following articles shall be exempt from the provisions of this Act, viz: sugar, rice, coffeee, tea. . . .

SECTION 4. The Collector shall collect the Chinese police tax, provided for in this Act, from all person liable to pay the same, and may seize the personal property of any such person refusing to pay such tax, and sell the same at public auction, by giving notice by proclamation one hour previous to such sale; and shall deliver the property, together with a bill of sale thereof, to the person agreeing to pay, and paying, the highest therefor, which delivery and bill of sale shall transfer to such person a good and sufficient title to the property. And after deducting the tax and necessary expenses incurred by reason of such refusal, seizure, and sale of property, the Collector shall return the surplus of the proceeds of the sale, if any, to the person whose property was sold; provided, That should any person, liable to pay the tax imposed in this Act, in any county in this State, escape into any other County, with the intention to evade the payment of such tax, then, and in that event, it shall be lawful for the Collector to pursue such person, and enforce the payment of such tax in the same manner as if no such escape had been made. And the Collector, when he shall collect Chinese police taxes, as provided for in this section, shall deliver to each of the persons paying such taxes a police tax receipt, with the blanks properly filled; provided, further, That any Mongolian, or Mongolians, may pay the above named tax to the County Treasurer, who is hereby authorized to receipt for the same in the same manner as the Collector. And any Mongolian, so paying said tax to the Treasurer of the County, if paid monthly, shall be entitled to a reduction of twenty percent on said tax. And if paid in advance for the year next ensuing, such Mongolian, or Mongolians, shall be entitled to a reduction of thirty-three and one third percent on said tax. But in all cases where the County Treasurer receipts for said tax yearly in advance, he shall do it by issuing receipts for each month separately; and any Mongolian who shall exhibit a County Treasurer's receipt, as above provided, to the Collector, shall be exempted from the payment of said tax to the Collector for the month for which said receipt was given.

SECTION 5. Any person charged with the collection of Chinese police taxes, who shall give any receipt other than the one prescribed in this Act, or receive money for such taxes without giving the necessary receipt therefor, or who shall insert more than one name in any receipt, shall be guilty of a felony, and, upon conviction thereof, shall be fined in a sum not exceeding one thousand dollars, and be imprisoned in the State Prison for a period not exceeding one year.

SECTION 6. Any Tax Collector who shall sell, or cause to be sold, any police tax receipt, with the date of the sale left blank, or which shall not be dated and signed, and blanks filled with ink, by the Controller, Auditor, and Tax Collector, and any person who shall make any alteration, or cause the same to be made, in any police tax receipt, shall be deemed guilty of a felony, and, on conviction therof, shall be fined in a sum not exceeding one thousand dollars, and imprisoned in the State prison for a period not exceeding 2 years; and the police tax receipt so sold, with blank date, or which shall not be signed and dated, and blanks filled with ink, as aforesaid, or which shall have been altered, shall be received in evidence in any Court of competent jurisdiction.

SECTION 7. Any person or company who shall hire persons liable to pay the Chinese police tax shall be held responsible for the payment of the tax due from each person so hired; and no employer shall be released from this liability on the ground that the employee is indebted to him (the employer), and the Collector may proceed against any such employer in the same manner as he might against the original party owing the taxes. The Collector shall have power to require any person or company believed to be indebted to, or to have any money, gold dust, or property of any kind, belonging to any person liable for police taxes, or in which such person is interested, in his or their possession, or under his or their control, to answer, under oath, as to such indebtedness, or the possession of such money, gold dust, or other property. In case a party is indebted, or has possession or control of any moneys, gold dust, or other property, as aforesaid, of such person liable for police taxes, he may collect from such party the amount of such taxes, and may require the delivery of such money, gold dust, or other property, as aforesaid; and in all cases the receipt of the Collector to said party shall be a complete bar to any demand made against said party, or his legal representatives, for the amounts of money, gold dust, or property, embraced therein.

SECTION 8. The Collector shall receive for his service, in collecting police taxes, twenty percent of all moneys which he shall collect from persons owing such taxes. And of the residue, after deducting the percentage of the Collector, forty percent shall be paid into the County Treasury, for the use of the State, forty percent into the general County Fund, for the use of the County, and the remaining twenty percent into the School Fund, for the benefit of schools within the County; provided, That in counties where the Tax Collector receives a specific salary, he shall not be required to pay the percentage allowed for collecting the police tax into the County Treasury, but shall be allowed to retain the same for his own use and benefit; provided, That where he shall collect the police tax by Deputy, the percentage shall go to the Deputy. . . .

SECTION 10. It is hereby made the duty of the various officers charged with the execution of the provisions of this Act, to carry out said provisions by themselves of Deputies; and for the faithful performance of their duties in the premises, they shall be liable on their official bonds, respectively. The Treasurers of the respective counties shall make their statements and settlements under this Act with the Controller of State, at the same times and in the same manner they make their settlements under the general Revenue Act.

SECTION 11. This Act shall take effect and be in force from and after the first day of May, next ensuing.

Document 4

THE CONSTITUTION OF THE STATE OF CALIFORNIA
1879

SECTION 1.   The Legislature shall prescribe all necessary regulations for the protection of the State, and the counties, cities, and towns thereof, from the burdens and evils arising from the presence of aliens, who are or may become vagrants, paupers, mendicants, criminals, or invalids afflicted with contagious or infectious diseases, and from aliens otherwise dangerous or detrimental to the well being or peace of the State, and to impose conditions upon which such persons may reside in the State, and to provide the means and mode of their removal from the State upon failure or refusal to comply with such conditions; provided, That nothing contained in this section shall be construed to impair or limit the power of the Legislature to pass such police laws or other regulations as it may deem necessary.

SECTION 2.   No corporation now existing or hereafter formed under the laws of this State shall, after the adoption of this Constitution, employ, directly or indirectly, in any capacity, any Chinese or Mongolian. The Legislature shall pass such laws as may be necessary to enforce this provision.

SECTION 3.   No Chinese shall be employed on any State, County, municipal, or other public work, except in punishment for crime.

SECTION 4.   The presence of foreigners ineligible to become citizens of the United States is declared to be dangerous to the well being of the State, and the Legislature shall discourage their immigration by all means within its power. Asiatic coolieism is a form of human slavery, and is forever prohibited in this State; and all contracts for coolie labor shall be void. All companies or corporations, whether formed in this country or any foreign country, for the importation of such labor, shall be subject to such penalties as the Legislature may prescribe. The Legislature shall delegate all necessary power to the incororated cities and towns of this State for the removal of Chinese without the limits of such cities and towns, or for their location within prescribed portions of those limits; and it shall also provide the necessary legislation to prohibit the introduction into this State of Chinese after the adoption of this Constitution. This section shall be enforced by appropriate legislation.

Document 5

AN ACT TO EXECUTE CERTAIN TREATY STIPULATIONS RELATING TO CHINESE
May 6, 1882

WHEREAS, In the opinion of the Government of the United States, the coming of Chinese laborers to this country endangers the good order of certain localities within the territory thereof: Therefore,

Be it enacted by the Senate and House of Representatives of the United States of America in Congress assembled, That from and after the expiration of ninety days next after the passage of this Act, and until the expiration of ten years·next after the passage of this Act, the coming of Chinese laborers to the United States be, and the same is hereby, suspended; and during such suspension it shall not be lawful for any Chinese laborer to come, or, having so come after the expiration of said ninety days, to remain within the United States.

SECTION 2. That the master of any vessel who shall knowingly bring within the United States on such vessel, and land or permit to be landed, any Chinese laborer, from any foreign port or place, shall be deemed guilty of a misdemeanor, and on conviction thereof shall be punished by a fine of not more than five hundred dollars for each and every such Chinese laborer so brought, and may be also imprisoned for a term not exceeding one year.

SECTION 3. That the two foregoing sections shall not apply to Chinese laborers who were in the United States on the seventeenth day of November, eighteen hundred and eighty, or who shall have come into the same before the expiration of ninety days next after the passage of this Act, and who shall produce to such master before going on board such vessel, and shall produce to the Collector of the port in the United States at which such vessel shall arrive, the evidence hereinafter in this Act required of his being one of the laborers in this section mentioned; nor shall the two foregoing sections apply to the case of any master, whose vessel, being bound to a port not within the United States, shall come within the jurisdiction of the United States by reason of being in distress or in stress of weather, or touching at any port of the United States on its voyage to any foreign port or place: Provided, That all Chinese laborers brought on such vessel shall depart with the vessel on leaving port.

SECTION 4. That for the purpose of properly identifying Chinese laborers who were in the United States on the seventeenth day of November, eighteen hundred and eighty, or who shall have come into the same before the expiration of ninety days next after the passage of this Act, and in order to furnish them with the proper evidence of their right to go from and come to the United States of their free will and accord, as provided by the treaty between the United States and China dated November seventeenth, eighteen hundred and eighty, the Collector of Customs of the district from which any such Chinese laborer shall depart from the United States shall, in person or by Deputy, go on board each vessel having on board any such Chinese laborer and cleared or about to sail from his district for a foreign port, and on such vessel make a list of all such Chinese laborers, which shall be entered in registry books to be kept for that purpose, in which shall be stated the name, age, occupation, last place of residence, physical marks or peculiarities, and all facts necessary for the identification of each of such Chinese laborers, which books shall be safely kept in the custom house; and every such Chinese laborer so departing from the United States shall be entitled to, and shall receive, free of any charge or cost upon application therefor, from the Collector or his Deputy, at the time such list is taken, a certificate, signed by the Collector or his Deputy and attested by his seal of office in such form as the Secretary of the Treasury shall prescribe, which certificate shall contain a statement of the name, age, occupation, last place of residence, personal description, and facts of identification of the Chinese laborer to whom the certificate is issued, corresponding with the said list and registry in all particulars. In case any Chinese laborer after having received such certificate shall leave such vessel before her departure he shall deliver his certificate to the master of the vessel, and if such Chinese laborer shall fail to return to such vessel before her departure from port the certificate shall be delivered by the master to the Collector of Customs for cancellation. The certificate herein provided for shall entitle the Chinese laborer to whom the same is issued to return to and reenter the United States upon producing and delivering the same to the Collector of Customs of the district at which such Chinese laborer shall seek to reenter; and upon delivery of such certificate by such Chinese laborer to the Collector of Customs at the time of reentry in the United States, said Collector shall cause the same to be filed in the custom house and duly canceled.

SECTION 5. That any Chinese laborer mentioned in Section 4 of this Act being in the United States, and desiring to depart from the United States by land, shall have the right to demand and receive, free of charge or cost, a certificate of identification similar to that provided for in Section 4 of this Act to be issued to such Chinese laborers as may desire to leave the United States by water; and it is hereby made the duty of the Collector of Customs of the district next adjoining the foreign country to which said Chinese laborer desires to go to issue such certificate, free of charge or cost, upon application by such Chinese laborer, and to enter the same upon registry books to be kept by him for the purpose, as provided for in Section 4 of this Act.

SECTION 6. That in order to the faithful execution of Articles 1 and 2 of the treaty in this Act before mentioned, every Chinese person other than a laborer who may be entitled by said treaty and this Act to come within the United States, and who shall be about to come to the United States, shall be identified as so entitled by the Chinese Government in each case, such identity to be evidenced by a certificate issued under the authority of said Government, which certificate shall be in the English language or (if not English language) accompanied by a translation into English, stating such right to come, and which certificate shall state the name, title, or official rank, if any, the age, height, and all physical peculiarities, former and present occupation or profession, and place of residence in China of the person to whom the certificate is issued and that such person is entitled conformably to the treaty in this Act mentioned to come within the United States. Such certificate shall be prima facie evidence of the fact set forth therein, and shall be produced to the Collector of Customs, or his deputy, of the port in the district in the United States at which the person named therein shall arrive.

SECTION 7. That any person who shall knowingly and falsely alter or substitute any name for the name written in such certificate or forge any such certificate, or knowingly utter any forged or fraudulent certificate, or falsely personate any person named in any such certificate, shall be deemed guilty of a misdemeanor; and upon conviction thereof shall be fined in a sum not exceeding one thousand dollars, and imprisoned in a penitentiary for a term of not more than five years.

SECTION 8. That the master of any vessel arriving in the United States from any foreign port or place shall, at the same time he delivers a manifest of the cargo, and if there be no cargo, then at the time of making a report of the entry of the vessel pursuant of law, in addition to the other matter required to be reported, and before landing, or permitting to land, any Chinese passengers, deliver and report to the Collector of Customs of the district in which such vessel shall have arrived a separate list of all Chinese passengers taken on board his vessel at any foreign port or place, and all such passengers on board the vessel at that time. Such lists shall show the names of such passengers (and if accredited officers of the Chinese Government traveling on the business of that Government, or their sevants, with a note of such facts), and the names and other particulars, as shown by their respective certificates; and such list shall be sworn to by the master in the manner required by law in relation to the manifest of the cargo. Any willful refusal or neglect of any such master to comply with the provisions of this section shall incur the same penalties and forfeiture as are provided for a refusal or neglect to report and deliver a manifest of the cargo.

SECTION 9. That before any Chinese passengers are landed from any such vessel, the Collector or his Deputy shall proceed to examine such passengers, comparing the certificates with the list and with the passengers; and no passenger shall be allowed to land in the United States from such vessel in violation of the law.

SECTION 10. That every vessel whose master shall knowingly violate any of the provisions of this Act shall be deemed forfeited to the United States, and shall be liable to seizure and condemnation in any district of the United States into which such vessel may enter or in which she may be found.

SECTION 11. That any person who shall knowingly bring into or cause to be brought into the United States by land, or who shall knowingly aid or abet the same, or aid or abet the landing in the United States from any vessel of any Chinese person not lawfully entitled to enter the United States, shall be deemed guilty of a misdemeanor, and shall, on conviction thereof, be fined in a sum not exceeding one thousand dollars, and imprisoned for a term not exceeding one year.

SECTION 12. That no Chinese person shall be permitted to enter the United States by land without producing to the proper officer of customs, the certificate in this act required of Chinese persons seeking to land from a vessel. And any Chinese person found unlawfully within the United States shall be caused to be removed therefrom to the country from whence he came, by direction of the President of the United States, and at the cost of the United States, after being brought before some justice, judge, or commissioner of a Court of the United States and found to be one not lawfully entitled to remain in the United States.

SECTION 13. That this Act shall not apply to diplomatic and other officers of the Chinese Government traveling upon the business of that Government, whose credentials shall be taken as equivalent to the certificate in this Act mentioned, and shall exempt them and their body and household servants from the provisions of this Act as to other Chinese persons.

SECTION 14. That hereafter no State Court or Court of the United States shall admit Chinese to citizenship; and all laws in conflict with this Act are hereby repealed.

SECTION 15. That the words "Chinese laborers" wherever used in this Act, shall be construed to mean both skilled and unskilled laborers and Chinese employed in mining.

Document 6

AN ACT TO AMEND AN ACT ENTITLED "AN ACT TO EXECUTE CERTAIN TREATY STIPULATIONS RELATING TO CHINESE," APPROVED MAY SIXTH, EIGHTEEN HUNDRED AND EIGHTY-TWO
July 5, 1884

Be it enacted by the Senate and House of Representatives of the United States of America in Congress assembled, That Section 1 of the Act entitled "An Act to Execute Certain Treaty Stipulations Relating to Chinese", approved May sixth, eighteen hundred and eighty-two, is hereby amended so as to read as follows:

WHEREAS, in the opinion of the Government of the United States the coming of Chinese laborers to this country endangers the good order of certain localities within the territory thereof: Therefore

"Be it enacted by the Senate and House of Representatives of the United States of America in Congress assembled, That from and after the passage of this Act, and until the expiration of ten years next after the passage of this Act, the coming of Chinese laborers to the United States be, and the same is hereby, suspended, and during such suspension it shall not be lawful for any Chinese laborer to come from any foreign port or place, or having so come to remain within the United States."

Section 2 of said Act is hereby amended so as to read as follows:

"SECTION 2. That the master of any vessel who shall knowingly bring within the United States on such vessel, and land, or attempt to land, or permit to be landed any Chinese laborer, from any foreign port or place, shall be deemed guilty of a misdemeanor, and, on conviction thereof, shall be punished by a fine of not more than five hundred dollars for each and every such Chinese laborer so brought, and may also be imprisoned for a term not exceeding one year."

Section 3 of said Act is hereby amended so as to read as follows:

"SECTION 3. That the two foregoing sections shall not apply to Chinese laborers who were in the United States on the seventeenth day of November, eighteen hundred and eighty, or who shall have come into the same before the expiration of ninety days next after the passage of the Act to which this Act is amendatory, nor shall said sections apply to Chinese laborers who shall produce to such master before going on board such vessel, and shall produce to the Collector of the port in the United States at which such vessel shall arrive, the evidence hereinafter in this act required of his

being one of the laborers in this section mentioned; nor shall the two foregoing sections apply to the case of any master whose vessel, being bound
to a port not within the United States, shall come within the jursidiction of
the United States by reason of being in distress or in stress of weather, or
touching at any port of the United States on its voyage to any foreign port or
place: Provided, That all Chinese laborers brought on such vessel shall not
be permitted to land except in case of absolute necessity, and must depart
with the vessel on leaving port."

Section 4 of said Act is hereby amended so as to read as follows:

"SECTION 4. That for the purpose of properly identifying Chinese laborers who were in the United States on the seventeenth day of November,
eighteen hundred and eighty, or who shall have come into the same before
the expiration to ninety days next after the passage of the Act to which this
Act is amendatory, and in order to furnish them with the proper evidence
of their right to go from and come to the United States as provided by the
said Act and the treaty between the United States and China dated November
seventeenth, eighteen hundred and eighty, the Collector of Customs of the
district from which any such Chinese laborer shall depart from the United
States shall, in person or by Deputy, go on board each vessel having on
board any such Chinese laborer, and cleared or about to sail from his district for a foreign port, and on such vessel make a list of all such Chinese
laborers which shall be entered in registry books to be kept for that purpose, in which shall be stated the individual, family, and tribal name in
full, the age, occupation, when and where followed, last place of residence,
physical marks or peculiarities, and all facts necessary for the identification of each such Chinese laborer, which books shall be safely kept in the
custom house; and every such Chinese laborer so departing from the United
States shall be entitled to and shall receive, free of any charge or cost upon application therefor, from the Collector or his Deputy, in the name of
said Collector and attested by said Collector's seal of office at the time
such list is taken, a certificate, signed by the Collector or his Deputy and
attested by his seal or office, in such form as the Secretary of the Treasury shall prescribe, which certificate shall contain a statement of the individual, family, and tribal name in full; age, occupation, when and where
followed, of the Chinese laborer to whom the certificate is issued, corresponding with the said list and registry in all particulars. In case any Chinese laborer, after having received such certificate, shall leave such vessel before her departure, he shall deliver his certificate to the master of
the vessel; and if such Chinese laborer shall fail to return to such vessel
before her departure from port, the certificate shall be delivered by the
master to the Collector of Customs for cancellation. The certificate herein provided for shall entitle the Chinese laborer to whom the same is issued
to return to and reenter the United States upon producing and delivering the
same to the Collector of Customs of the district at which such Chinese laborer shall seek to reenter, and said certificate shall be the only evidence
permissible to establish his right of reentry; and upon delivering of such

certificate by such Chinese laborer to the Collector of Customs at the time of reentry in the United States, said Collector shall cause the same to be filed in the custom house and duly canceled."

Section 6 of said Act is hereby amended so as to read as follows:

"SECTION 6. That in order to the faithful execution of the provisions of this Act, every Chinese person other than a laborer, who may be entitled by said treaty or this Act to come within the United States, and who shall be about to come to the United States, shall obtain the permission of and be identified as so entitled by the Chinese Government, or of such other foreign government of which at the time such Chinese person shall be a subject, in each case to be evidenced by a certificate issued by such government, which certificate shall be in the English language and shall show such permission, with the name of the permitted person in his or her proper signature, and which certificate shall state the individual, family, and tribal name in full, title or official rank, if any, the age, height, and all physical peculiarities, former and present occupation or profession, when and where and how long pursued, and place of residence of the person to whom the certificate is issued, and that such person is entitled by this Act to come within the United States. If the person so applying for a certificate shall be a merchant, said certificate shall, in addition to above requirements, state the nature, character, and estimated value of the business carried on by him prior to and at the same time of his application as aforesaid: Provided, That nothing in this Act nor in said treaty shall be construed as embracing within the meaning of the word 'merchant' hucksters, peddlers, or those engaged in taking, drying, or otherwise preserving shell or other fish for home consumption or exportation. If the certificate be sought for the purpose of travel for curiosity, it shall also state whether the applicant intends to pass through or travel within the United States, together with his financial standing in the country from which such certificate is desired. The certificate provided for in this Act, and the identity of the person named therein, shall, before such person goes on board any vessel to proceed to the United States, be vised by the endorsement of the diplomatic representative, or of the consular representative of the United States at the port or place from which the person named in the certificate is about to depart; and such diplomatic representative whose endorsement is so required is hereby empowered, and it shall be his duty, before endorsing such certificate as aforesaid, to examine into the truth of the statement set forth in said certificate, and if he shall find upon examination that said or any of the statements therein contained are untrue it shall be his duty to refuse to endorse the same. Such certificate vised as aforesaid shall be <u>prima facie</u> evidence of the facts set forth therein, and shall be produced to the Collector of Customs of the port in the district in the United States at which the person named therein shall arrive, and afterward produced to the proper authorities of the United States whenever lawfully demanded, and shall be the sole evidence permissible on the part of the person so producing the same to establish a right of entry into the United States; but said certificate may be controverted and the facts therein disproved by the United States authorities."

Section 8 of said Act is hereby amended so as to read as follows:

"SECTION 8. That the master of any vessel arriving in the United States from any foreign port or place shall, at the same time he delivers a manifest of the cargo, and if there be no cargo, then at the time of making a report of the entry of the vessel pursuant to law in addition to the other matter required to be reported, and before landing, or permitting to land, any Chinese passengers, deliver and report to the Collector of Customs of the district in which such vessel shall have arrived a separate list of all Chinese passengers taken on board his vessel at any foreign port or place, and all such passengers on board the vessel at that time. Such list shall show the names of such passengers (and if accredited officers of the Chinese or of any other foreign government, traveling on the business of that government, or their servants, with a note of such facts) and the names and other particulars as shown by their respective certificates; and such list shall be sworn to by the master in the manner required by law in relation to the manifest of the cargo. Any refusal or willful neglect of any such master to comply with the provisions of this section shall incur the same penalties and forfeiture as are provided for a refusal or neglect to report and deliver a manifest of the cargo."

Section 10 of said Act is hereby amended so as to read as follows:

"SECTION 10. That every vessel whose master shall knowingly violate any of the provisions of this Act shall be deemed forfeited to the United States, and shall be liable to seizure and condemnation in any district of the United States into which such vessel may enter or in which she may be found."

Section 11 of said Act is hereby amended so as to read as follows:

"SECTION 11. That any person who shall knowingly bring into or cause to be brought into the United States by land, or who shall aid or abet the same, or aid or abet the landing in the United States from any vessel, of any Chinese person not lawfully entitled to enter the United States, shall be deemed guilty of a misdemeanor, and shall, on conviction thereof, be fined in a sum not exceeding one thousand dollars, and imprisoned for a term not exceeding one year."

Section 12 of said Act is hereby amended so as to read as follows:

"SECTION 12. That no Chinese person shall be permitted to enter the United States by land without producing to the proper officer of customs the certificate in this Act required of Chinese persons seeking to land from a vessel; and any Chinese person found unlawfully within the United States shall be caused to be removed therefrom to the country from whence he came, and at the cost of the United States, after being brought before some justice, judge, or commissioner of a Court of the United States and found to be one not lawfully entitled to be or to remain in the United States; and in all such cases the person who brought or aided in bringing such person to the United States shall be liable to the Government of the United States for all necessary expenses incurred in such investigation and removal; and all peace officers of the several States and Territories of the United States are hereby invested with the same authority as a marshal or United States marshal in reference to carrying out the provisions of this Act or the Act of which this is amendatory, as a marshal or deputy marshal of the United States, and shall be entitled to like compensation to be audited and paid by the same officers; and the United States shall pay all costs and charges for the maintenance and return of any Chinese person having the certificate prescribed by law as entitling such Chinese person to come into the United States who may not have been permitted to land from any vessel by reason of any provisions of this Act."

Section 13 of said Act is hereby amended so as to read as follows:

"SECTION 13.   That this Act shall not apply to diplomatic and other officers of the Chinese or other governments traveling upon the business of that government, whose credentials shall be taken as equivalent to the certificate in this Act mentioned, and shall exempt them and their body and household servants from the provisions of this Act as to other Chinese persons."

Section 15 of said Act is amended so as to read as follows:

"SECTION 15.   That the provisions of this Act shall apply to all subjects of China and Chinese, whether subjects of China or any other foreign power, and the words Chinese laborers, wherever used in this Act, shall be construed to mean both skilled and unskilled laborers and Chinese employed in mining."

SECTION 16.   That any violation of any of the provisions of this Act, or of the Act of which this is amendatory, the punishment of which is not otherwise herein provided for, shall be deemed a misdemeanor, and shall be punishable by a fine not exceeding one thousand dollars, or by imprisonment for not more than one year, or both such fine and imprisonment.

SECTION 17.   That nothing contained in this Act shall be construed to affect any prosectuion or other proceeding, criminal or civil, begun under the Act of which this is amendatory; but such prosecution or other proceeding, criminal or civil, shall proceed as if this Act had not been passed.

Document 7

AN ACT TO PROHIBIT THE COMING OF CHINESE
LABORERS TO THE UNITED STATES
September 13, 1888

Be it enacted by the Senate and House of Representatives of the United States of America in Congress assembled, That from and after the date of the exchange of ratifications of the pending treaty between the United States of America and His Imperial Majesty the Emperor of China, signed on the twelfth day of March, anno Domini eighteen hundred and eighty-eight, it shall be unlawful for any Chinese person, whether a subject of China or of any other power, to enter the United States, except as hereinafter provided.

SECTION 2. That Chinese officials, teachers, students, merchants, or travelers for pleasure or curiosity, shall be permitted to enter the United States, but in order to entitle themselves to do so, they shall first obtain the permission of the Chinese Government, or other Government of which they may at the time be citizens or subjects. Such permission and also their personal identity shall in such case be evidenced by a certificate to be made out by the diplomatic representative of the United States in the country, or of the consular representative of the United States at the port or place from which the person named therein comes. The certificate shall contain a full description of such person, of his age, height, and general physical features, and shall state his former and present occupation or profession and place of residence, and shall be made out in duplicate. One copy shall be delivered open to the person named and described, and the other copy shall be sealed up and delivered by the diplomatic or consular officer as aforesaid to the captain of the vessel on which the person named in the certificate sets sail for the United States, together with the sealed certificate, which shall be addressed to the Collector of Customs at the port where such person is to land. There shall be delivered to the aforesaid captain a letter from the consular officer addressed to the Collector of Customs aforesaid, and stating that said consular officer has on a certain day delivered to the said captain a certificate of the right of the person named therein to enter the United States as a Chinese official, or other exempted person, as the case may be. And any captain who lands or attempts to land a Chinese person in the United States, without having in his possession a sealed certificate, as required in this section, shall be liable to the penalties prescribed in Section 9 of this Act.

SECTION 3. That the provisions of this Act shall apply to all persons of the Chinese race, whether subjects of China or other foreign power, excepting Chinese diplomatic or consular officers and their attendants; and the words "Chinese laborers", whenever used in this Act, shall be construed to mean both skilled and unskilled laborers and Chinese employed in mining.

SECTION 4. That the master of any vessel arriving in the United States from any foreign port or place with any Chinese passengers on board shall, when he delivers his manifest of cargo, and if there be no cargo, when he makes legal entry of his vessel, and before landing or permitting to land any Chinese person (unless a diplomatic or consular officer, or attendant of such officer), deliver to the Collector of Customs of the district in which the vessel shall have arrived the sealed certificates and letters as aforesaid, and a separate list of all Chinese persons taken on board of his vessel at any foreign port or place, and of all such persons on board at the time of arrival as aforesaid. Such list shall show the names of such persons and other particulars as shown by their open certificates, or other evidences required by this Act, and such list shall be sworn to by the master in the manner required by law in relation to the manifest of the cargo.

The master of any vessel as aforesaid shall not permit any Chinese diplomatic or consular officer or attendant of such officer to land without having first been informed by the Collector of Customs of the official character of such officer or attendant. Any refusal or willful neglect of the master of any vessel to comply with the provisions of this section shall incur the same penalties and forfeitures as are provided for a refusal or neglect to report and deliver a manifest of the cargo.

SECTION 5. That from and after the passage of this Act, no Chinese laborer in the United States shall be permitted, after having left, to return thereto, except under the conditions stated in the following sections.

SECTION 6. That no Chinese laborer within the purview of the preceding section shall be permitted to return to the United States unless he has a lawful wife, child, or parent in the United States, or property therein of the value of one thousand dollars, or debts of like amount due him and pending settlement. The marriage to such wife must have taken place at least a year prior to the application of the laborer for a permit to return to the United States, and must have been followed by the continuous cohabitation of the parties as man and wife.

If the right to return be claimed on the grounds of property or of debts, it must appear that the property is bona fide and not colorably acquired for the purpose of evading this Act, or that the debts are unascertained and unsettled, and not promissory notes or other similar acknowledgements of ascertained liability.

SECTION 7. That a Chinese person claiming the right to be permitted to leave the United States and return thereto on any of the grounds stated in the foregoing section, shall apply to the Collector of Customs of the district

from which he wishes to depart at least a month prior to the time of his departure, and shall make on oath before said Collector a full statement de-
scriptive of his family, or property, or debts, as the case may be, and
shall furnish to said Collector such proofs of the facts entitling him to return as shall be required by the rules and regulations prescribed from
time to time by the Secretary of the Treasury, and for any false swearing
in relation thereto he shall incur the penalties of perjury. He shall also
permit the Collector to take a full description of his person, which description the Collector shall retain and mark with a number. And if the Collector, after hearing the proofs and investigating all the circumstances of the
case, shall decide to issue a certificate of return, he shall at such time
and place as he may designate, sign and give to the person applying a certificate containing the number of the description last aforesaid, which shall
be the sole evidence given to such person of his right to return. If this
last named certificate be transferred, it shall become void, and the person
to whom it was given shall forfeit his right to return to the United States. . . .

SECTION 15. That the Act entitled "An Act to Execute Certain Treaty
Stipulations Relating to Chinese, " approved May sixth, eighteen hundred
and eighty-two, and an act to amend said act approved July fifth, eighteen
hundred and eighty-four, are hereby repealed to take effect upon the ratifi-
cation of the pending treaty as provided in section one of this act.

Document 8

AN ACT TO SUPPLEMENT AN ACT ENTITLED "AN ACT TO EXECUTE
CERTAIN TREATY STIPULATIONS RELATING TO CHINESE,"
APPROVED THE SIXTH DAY OF MAY, EIGHTEEN HUNDRED AND
EIGHTY-TWO

October 1, 1888

Be it enacted by the Senate and House of Representatives of the United
States of America in Congress assembled, That from and after the passage
of this Act, it shall be unlawful for any Chinese laborer who shall at any
time heretofore have been, or who may now or hereafter be, a resident
within the United States, and who shall have departed, or shall depart,
therefrom, and shall not have returned before the passage of this Act, to
return to, or remain in, the United States.

SECTION 2. That no certificates of identity provided for in the fourth
and fifth sections of the Act of which this is a supplement shall hereafter
be issued; and every certificate heretofore issued in pursuance thereof is
hereby declared void and of no effect, and the Chinese laborer claiming admission by virtue thereof shall not be permitted to enter the United States.

SECTION 3. That all the duties prescribed, liabilities, penalties, and
forfeitures imposed, and the powers conferred by the second, tenth, eleventh, and twelfth sections of the Act to which this is a supplement are hereby extended and made applicable to the provision of this Act.

SECTION 4. That all such part or parts of the Act to which this is a
supplement as are inconsistent herewith are hereby repealed.

Document 9

AN ACT TO PROHIBIT THE COMING OF CHINESE PERSONS INTO THE UNITED STATES
May 5, 1892

Be it enacted by the Senate and House of Representatives of the United States of America in Congress assembled, That all laws now in force prohibiting and regulating the coming into this country of Chinese persons and persons of Chinese descent are hereby continued in force for a period of ten years from the passage of this Act.

SECTION 2. That any Chinese person or person of Chinese descent, when convicted and adjudged under any of said laws to be not lawfully entitled to be or remain in the United States, shall be removed from the United States to China, unless he or they shall make it appear to the justice, judge, or commissioner before whom he or they are tried that he or they are subjects or citizens of some other country, in which case he or they shall be removed from the United States to such country: Provided, That in any case where such other country of which such Chinese person shall claim to be a citizen or subject shall demand any tax as a condition of the removal of such person to that country, he or she shall be removed to China.

SECTION 3. That any Chinese person or person of Chinese descent arrested under the provisions of this Act or the Acts hereby extended shall be adjudged to be unlawfully within the United States unless such person shall establish, by affirmative proof, to the satisfaction of such justice, judge or commissioner, his lawful right to remain in the United States.

SECTION 4. That any such Chinese person or person of Chinese descent convicted and adjudged to be not lawfully entitled to be or remain in the United States shall be imprisoned at hard labor for a period of not exceeding one year and thereafter removed from the United States, as hereinbefore provided.

SECTION 5. That after the passage of this Act, on an application to any judge, or Court of the United States in the first instance for a writ of habeas corpus, by a Chinese person seeking to land in the United States, to whom the privilege has been denied, no bail shall be allowed, and such application shall be heard and determined promptly without unnecessary delay.

SECTION 6. And it shall be the duty of all Chinese laborers within

the limits of the United States at the time of the passage of this Act, and
who are entitled to remain in the United States, to apply to the Collector
of Internal Revenue of their respective districts, within one year after the
passage of this Act, for a certificate of residence, and any Chinese laborer
within the limits of the United States who shall neglect, fail, or refuse to
comply with the provisions of this Act, or who, after one year from the
passage hereof, shall be found within the jurisdiction of the United States
without such certificate of residence, shall be deemed and adjudged to be
unlawfully within the United States, and may be arrested by any United
States customs official, Collector of Internal Revenue or his Deputies,
United States Marshal or his Deputies, and taken before a United States
Judge, whose duty it shall be to order that he be deported from the United
States as hereinbefore provided, unless he shall establish clearly to the
satisfaction of said Judge that by reason of accident, sickness, or other
unavoidable cause, he has been unable to procure his certificate, and to
the satisfaction of the Court, and by at least one credible white witness,
that he was a resident of the United States at the time of the passage of
this Act; and if upon the hearing it shall appear that he is so entitled to a
certificate, it shall be granted upon his paying the cost. Should it appear
that said Chinaman had procured a certificate which has been lost or destroyed, he shall be detained and judgement suspended a reasonable time to
enable him to procure a duplicate from the officer granting it, and in
such cases the cost of said arrest and trial shall be in the discretion of the
Court. And any Chinese person, other than a Chinese laborer, having a
right to be and remain in the United States, desiring such certificates as
evidence of such right, may apply for and receive the same without charge.

SECTION 7. That immediately after the passage of this Act the Secretary of the Treasury shall make such rules and regulations as may be necessary for the efficient execution of this Act, and shall prescribe the necessary forms and furnish the necessary blanks to enable Collectors of Internal Revenue to issue the certificates required hereby, and make such
provisions that certificates may be procured in localities convenient to the
applicants. Such certificates shall be issued without charge to the applicant, and shall contain the name, age, local residence, and occupation of
the applicant, and such other description of the applicant as shall be prescribed by the Secretary of the Treasury, and a duplicate thereof shall be
filed in the office of the Collector of Internal Revenue for the district within which such Chinaman makes applications.

SECTION 8. That any person who shall knowingly and falsely alter or
substitute any name for the name written in such certificate or forged certificate, or knowingly utter any forged or fraudulent certificate, or falsely
personate any person named in such certificate, shall be guilty of a misdemeanor, and upon conviction thereof shall be fined in a sum not exceeding one thousand dollars or imprisoned in the penitentiary for a term of

not more than five years.

SECTION 9. The Secretary of the Treasury may authorize the payment of such compensation in the nature of fees to the Collectors of Internal Revenue, for services performed under the provisions of this Act, in addition to salaries now allowed by law, as he shall deem necessary, not exceeding the sum of one dollar for each certificate issued.

Document 10

JOINT RESOLUTION OF CONGRESS EXTENDING ANTI-CHINESE LEGISLATION TO HAWAII
July 7, 1898

There shall be no further immigration of Chinese into the Hawaiian Islands, except upon such conditions as are now or may hereafter be allowed by the laws of the United States; and no Chinese, by reason of anything herein contained, shall be allowed to enter the United States from the Hawaiian Islands.

Document 11

AN ACT TO PROVIDE A GOVERNMENT FOR THE TERRITORY OF HAWAII
April 30, 1900

SECTION 4. That all persons who were citizens of the Republic of Hawaii on August 12, 1898, are hereby declared to be citizens of the United States and citizens of the Territory of Hawaii.

SECTION 101. That Chinese in the Hawaiian Islands when this Act has taken effect may within one year thereafter obtain certificates of residence as required by "An Act to Prohibit the Coming of Chinese Persons into the United States," approved November 3, 1893, entitled "An Act to Amend an Act Entitled 'An Act to Prohibit the Coming of Chinese Persons into the United States,'" approved May 5, 1892, and until the expiration of said year shall not be deemed to be unlawfully in the United States if found therein without such certificates. Provided, however, That no Chinese laborer, whether he shall hold such certificate or not, shall be allowed to enter any State, Territory, or District of the United States from the Hawaiian Islands.

Document 12

AN ACT TO PROHIBIT THE COMING INTO AND TO REGULATE THE
RESIDENCE WITHIN THE UNITED STATES, ITS TERRITORIES
AND ALL TERRITORY UNDER ITS JURISDICTION, AND THE
DISTRICT OF COLUMBIA, OF CHINESE AND PERSONS OF
CHINESE DESCENT
April 29, 1902

Be it enacted by the Senate and House of Representatives of the United
States of America in Congress assembled, That all laws now in force prohibiting and regulating the coming of Chinese persons, and persons therein,
including Sections five, six, seven, eight, nine, ten, eleven, thirteen, and
fourteen of the Act entitled "An Act to Prohibit the Coming of Chinese Laborers into the United States," approved September thirteenth, eighteen
hundred and eighty-eight, be, and the same are hereby, reenacted, extended, and continued so far as the same are not inconsistent with treaty
obligations, until otherwise provided by law, and said laws shall also apply
to the island territory under the jurisdiction of the United States, and prohibit the immigration of Chinese laborers, not citizens of the United States,
whether in such island territory at the time of cession or not, and from one
portion of the island territory of the United States to another portion of said
island territory: Provided, however, That said laws shall not apply to the
transit of Chinese laborers from one island to another island of the same
group; and any islands within the jurisdiction of any State or the District of
Alaska shall be considered a part of the mainland under this section.

SECTION 2. That the Secretary of the Treasury is hereby authorized
and empowered to make and prescribe, and from time to time to change,
such rules and regulations not inconsistent with the laws of the land as he
may deem necessary and proper to execute the provision of this Act and of
the Acts hereby extended and continued and of the treaty of December eighth,
eighteen hundred and ninety-four, between the United States and China, and
with the approval of the President to appoint such agents as he may deem
necessary for the efficient execution of said treaty and said Acts.

SECTION 3. That nothing in the provisions of this Act or any other
Act shall be construed to prevent, hinder, or restrict any foreign exhibitor,
representative, or citizen of any foreign nation, or the holder, who is a
citizen of any foreign nation, of any concession or privilege from any fair
or exposition authorized by Act of Congress from bringing into the United
States under contract, such mechanics, artisans, agents, or other em-
ployees, natives of their respective foreign countries, as they or any of
them may deem necessary for the purpose of making preparation for in-

stalling or conducting their exhibits or of preparing for installing or conducting any business authorized or permitted under or by virtue of or pertaining to any concession or privilege which may have been or may be
granted by any said fair or exposition in connection with such exposition,
under such rules and regulations as the Secretary of the Treasury may prescribe, both as to the admission and return of such person or persons.

SECTION 4. That it shall be the duty of every Chinese laborer, other
than a citizen, rightfully in, and entitled to remain in any of the insular
territory of the United States (Hawaii excepted) at the time of the passage
of this Act, to obtain within one year thereafter a certificate of residence
in the insular territory wherein he resides, which certificate shall entitle
him to reside therein, and upon failure to obtain such certificate as herein provided he shall be deported from such insular territory; and the Philippine Commission is authorized and required to make all regulations and
provisions necessary for the enforcement of this section in the Philippine
Islands, including the form and substance of the certificate of residence
so that the same shall clearly and sufficiently identify the holder thereof
and enable officials to prevent fraud in the transfer of the same: Provided,
however, That if said Philippine Commission shall find that it is impos-
sible to complete the registration herein provided for within one year of
passage of this Act, said Commission is hereby authorized and empowered
to extend the time for such registration for a further period not exceeding
one year.

Document 13

REGULATIONS GOVERNING THE ADMISSION OF CHINESE
February 26, 1907

Rule 3. Chinese aliens shall be examined as to their right to admission to the United States under the provision of the law regulating immigration as well as under the laws relating to the exclusion of Chinese. As the immigration acts relate to aliens in general, the status of Chinese applying for admission must first be determined in accordance with the terms of that law and of the regulation drawn in pursuance thereof; then, if found admissible under such laws, and regulations, their status under the Chinese exclusion laws and regulations shall be determined. In order to avoid inconvenience, delay, or annoyance to Chinese applicants arising through misunderstanding, and in the interest of good administration, examination under both sets of laws and regulations shall be made, in the order stated, duly at the ports named in Rule 4 hereof.

Rule 5. Immediately upon arrival of Chinese persons at any port mentioned in Rule 4, it shall be the duty of the officer in charge of the administration of Chinese exclusion laws to have said Chinese persons examined promptly, as by law provided, touching their right to admission; and to permit to land those proving such right: Provided, That nothing contained in these regulations shall be construed to authorize the boarding of vessels of foreign navies arriving at ports of the United States for the purpose of enforcing the provisions of the Chinese exclusion laws.

Rule 6. The examination prescribed in Rule 5 shall be separate and apart from the public, in the presence of Government officials and such other witnesses only as the examining officers shall designate; and all witnesses presenting themselves on behalf of any Chinese applicants shall be fully heard. If upon the conclusion of the hearing the Chinese applicant, if adjudged to be inadmissible, he shall be advised of his right of appeal by a notice written or printed in Chinese language, and his counsel shall be permitted, after notice of appeal has been duly filed, to examine and make copies of evidence upon which the excluding decision is based. If there is a consular officer of China at port where examination is held, he also shall be notified in writing that the said Chinese applicant has been refused a landing, and shall be permitted to examine the record.

Rule 7. Every Chinese person permitted to land from a vessel for examination at some designated port, or for immediate hospital treatment as provided in Rule 1, shall be considered as still on shipboard until finally and lawfully landed, so far as relates to the responsibility of the master, agents, or owner of such vessel for his safeguarding, maintenance, and hospital expenses.

Rule 9. Every Chinese person refused admission to the United States, being actually or constructively on the vessel or other conveyance by which he was brought to a port of entry, must be returned to the country whence he came, at the expense of the transportation agency owning such vessels or conveyance.

Rule 12. Every Chinese person refused admission under the provisions of the exclusion laws by the decision of the officer in charge at the port of entry may take an appeal to the Secretary of Commerce and Labor by giving written notice thereof to the officer in charge within two days, exclusive of Sundays and legal holidays, after such decision is rendered.

Document 14

AN ACT TO REPEAL THE CHINESE EXCLUSION ACTS, TO ESTABLISH QUOTAS, AND FOR OTHER PURPOSES
December 17, 1943

Be it enacted by the Senate and House of Representatives of the United States of America in Congress assembled, That the following Acts or parts of Acts relating to the exclusion or deportation of persons of the Chinese race are hereby repealed: May 6, 1882 (22 Stat L. 58); July 5, 1884 (23 Stat. L. 115); September 13, 1888 (25 Stat. L. 476); October 1, 1888 (25 Stat. L. 504); May 5, 1892 (27 Stat. L. 25); November 3, 1893 (28 Stat. L. 7); that portion of Section 1 of the Act of July 7, 1898 (30 Stat. L. 750, 751), which reads as follows: "There shall be no further immigration of Chinese into the Hawaiian Islands except upon such conditions as are now or may hereafter be allowed by the laws of the United States; and no other Chinese, by reason of anything herein contained, shall be allowed to enter the United States from the Hawaiian Islands"; Section 101 of the Act of April 30, 1900 (31 Stat. L. 141, 161); those portions of Section 1 of the Act of June 6, 1900 (31 Stat. L. 588, 611), which read as follows: "And nothing in Section 4 of the Act of August fifth, eighteen hundred and eighty-two (Twenty-second Statutes at Large, page two hundred and twenty-five), shall be construed to prevent the Secretary of the Treasury from hereafter detailing one officer employed in the enforcement of the Chinese Exclusion Acts for duty at the Treasury Department in Washington and hereafter the Commissioner-General of Immigration, in addition to his other duties, shall have charge of the administration of the Chinese exclusion law, under the supervision and direction of the Secretary of the Treasury"; March 3, 1901 (31 Stat. L. 1093); April 29, 1902 (32 Stat. L. 176); April 27, 1904 (33 Stat. L. 428); Section 25 of the Act of March 3, 1911 (36 Stat. L. 1087, 1094); that portion of the Act of August 24, 1912 (37 Stat. L. 417, 476), which reads as follows: "Provided, That all charges for maintenance or return of Chinese persons applying for admission to the United States shall hereafter be paid or reimbursed to the United States by the person, company, partnership, or corporation, bringing such Chinese to a port of the United States as applicants for admission"; that portion of the Act of June 23, 1913 (38 Stat. L. 4, 65), which reads as follows: "Provided, That from and after July first, nineteen hundred and thirteen all Chinese persons ordered deported under judicial writs shall be delivered by the Marshal of the district or his Deputy into the custody of any officer designated for that purpose by the Secretary of Commerce and Labor, for conveyance to the frontier or seaboard for deportation in the same manner as aliens deported under the immigration laws."

Section 2. With the exception of those coming under subsections (b), (d), (e), and (f) of Section 4, Immigration Act of 1924 (43 Stat. 155; 44 Stat. 812; 45 Stat. 1009; 46 Stat. 854; 47 Stat. 656; 8 U.S.C. 204), all Chinese persons entering the United States annually as immigrants shall be allocated to the quota for the Chinese computed under the provisions of Section 11 of the said Act. A preference up to 75 per centum of the quota shall be given to Chinese born and resident in China.

Section 3. Section 303 of the Nationality Act of 1940, as amended (54 Stat. 1140; 8 U.S.C. 703), is hereby amended by striking out the word "and" before the word "descendants", changing the colon after the word "Hemisphere" to a comma, and adding the following: "and Chinese persons or persons of Chinese descent."

B. TREATIES BETWEEN THE UNITED STATES AND CHINA

Document 15

THE TREATY OF PEACE, AMITY, AND COMMERCE BETWEEN THE UNITED STATES OF AMERICA AND THE CHINESE EMPIRE.

Signed at Wanghia, July 3, 1844
Ratifications exchanged at Canton, December 31, 1845

The United States of America and the Ta-Tsing Empire, desiring to establish firm, lasting, and sincere friendship between the two nations, having resolved to fix, in a manner clear and positive, by means of a Treaty or general convention of peace, amity, and commerce, the rules which shall in future be mutually observed in the intercourse of their respective countries; for which most desirable object the President of the United States has conferred full powers on their Commissioner, Caleb Cushing, Envoy Extraordinary and Minister Plenipotentiary of the United States to China, and the August Sovereign of the Ta-Tsing Empire, on his Minister and Commissioner Extraordinary, Kiyeng, of the Imperial House, a Vice-Guardian of the Heir Apparent, Governor-General of the Two Kwangs, and Superintendent-General of the Trade and Foreign Intercourse of the Five Ports:

And the said Commissioners, after having exchanged their said full powers and duly considered the premises, having agreed to the following Articles: --

Article I.

There shall be a perfect, permanent, and universal peace and a sincere and cordial amity between the United States of America on the one part, and the Ta-Tsing Empire on the other part, and between their people respectively, without exception of persons or places.

Article II.

Citizens of the United States resorting to China for the purpose of commerce will pay the duties of import and export prescribed by the Tariff which is fixed by and made a part of this Treaty. They shall in no case be subject to other or higher duties than are or shall be required of the people of any other nation whatever. Fees and charges of every sort are wholly abolished; and officers of the revenue who may be guilty of exaction shall be punished according to the laws of China. If the Chinese Government desire to modify in any respect the said Tariff, such modifications shall be made only in consultation with Consuls or other functionaries thereto duly authorized in behalf of the United States, and with consent thereof. And if additional advantages or privileges of whatever description be conceded hereafter by China to any other nation, the United States and the citizens thereof shall be entitled thereupon to a complete, equal, and impartial participation in the same.

Article III.

The citizens of the United States are permitted to frequent the five ports of Quangchow (Canton), Amoy, Fuchow, Ningpo, and Shanghai, and to reside with their families and trade there, and to proceed at pleasure with their vessels and merchandise to or from any Foreign port and either of the said five ports, and from either of said five ports to any other of them; but said vessels shall not unlawfully enter the other ports of China, nor carry on a clandestine and fraudulent trade along the coasts thereof; and any vessel belonging to a citizen of the United States which violates this provision shall, with her cargo, be subject to confiscation to the Chinese Government.

Article IV.

For the superintendence and regulation of the concerns of citizens of the United States doing business at the said five ports, the Government of the United States may appoint Consuls or other officers at the same, who shall be duly recognized as such by the officers of the Chinese Government, and shall hold official intercourse and correspondence with the latter, either personal or in writing, as occasion may require, on terms of equality and reciprocal respect. If disrespectfully treated or aggrieved in any way by the local authorities, the said officers, on the one hand, shall have the right to make representation of the same to the superior officers of the Chinese Government, who will see that full inquiry and strict justice be had in the premises; and on the other hand, the said Consuls will carefully avoid all acts of unnecessary offence to or collision with the officers and people of China.

Article V.

At each of the said five ports citizens of the United States lawfully engaged in commerce shall be permitted to import from their own or any other ports into China, and sell there, and purchase therein and export to their own or any other ports, all manner of merchandise of which the importation or exportation is not prohibited by this Treaty, paying the duties thereon which are prescribed by the Tariff hereinbefore established, and no other charges whatever....

Article XVI.

The Chinese Government will not hold itself responsible for any debts which may happen to be due from subjects of China to citizens of the United States, or for frauds committed by them, but citizens of the United States may seek redress in law; and on suitable representation being made to the Chinese local authorities through the Consul, they will cause due examination in the premises, and take all proper steps to compel satisfaction. But in case the debtor be dead, or without property, or have absconded, the creditor cannot be indemnified according to the old system of the cohong so called. And if citizens of the United States be indebted to subjects of China, the latter may seek redress in the same way through the Consul, but without any responsibility for the debt on the part of the United States.

Article XVII.

Citizens of the United States residing or sojourning at any of the ports open to Foreign commerce shall enjoy all proper accommodation in obtaining houses and places of business, or in hiring sites from the inhabitants on which to construct houses and places of business, and also hospitals, churches, and cemeteries. The local authorities of the two Governments shall select in concert the sites for the foregoing objects, having due regard to the feelings of the people in the location thereof; and the parties interested will fix the rent by mutual agreement, the proprietors on the one hand not demanding any exorbitant price, nor the merchants on the other unreasonably insisting on particular spots, but each conducting with justice and moderation; and any desecration of said cemeteries by subjects of China shall be severely punished according to law.

At the places of anchorage of the vessels of the United States, the citizens of the United States, merchants, seamen, or others sojourning there may pass and repass in the immediate neighborhood; but they shall not at their pleasure make excursions into the country among the villages at large, nor shall they repair to public marts for the purpose of disposing of goods unlawfully and in fraud of the revenue.

And in order to the preservation of the public peace, the local officers of Government at each of the five ports shall, in concert with the Consuls, define the limits beyond which it shall not be lawful for a citizen of the United States to go.

Article XVIII.

It shall be lawful for officers or citizens of the United States to employ scholars and people of any part of China, without distinction of persons, to teach any of the languages of the Empire, and to assist in literary labors, and the persons so employed shall not for that cause be subject to any injury on the part either of the Government or of individuals; and it shall in

like manner be lawful for citizens of the United States to purchase all manner of books in China.

Article XIX.

All citizens of the United States in China peaceably attending to their
affairs, being placed on a common footing of amity and goodwill with subjects of China, shall receive and enjoy, for themselves and everything ap-
pertaining to them, the special protection of the local authorities of Government, who shall defend them from all insult or injury of any sort on the
part of the Chinese.

If their dwellings or their property be threatened or attacked by mobs,
incendiaries, or other violent or lawless persons, the local officers, on
requisition of the Consul, will immediately despatch a military force to
disperse the rioters, and will apprehend the guilty individuals and punish
them with the utmost rigour of the law.

Article XX.

Citizens of the United States who may have imported merchandise into
any of the free ports of China, and paid the duty thereon, if they desire to
re-export the same in part or in whole to any other of the said ports, shall
be entitled to make application, through their Consul, to the Superintendent
of Customs, who, in order to prevent frauds on the revenue, shall cause
examination to be made by suitable officers to see that the duties paid on
such goods entered on the Custom House books correspond with the representation made, and that the goods remain with their original marks un-
changed and shall then make a memorandum in the port clearance of the
goods and the amount of duties paid on the same, and deliver the same to
the merchant, and shall also certify the facts to the officers of Customs of
the other ports.

All which being done, on the arrival in port of the vessel in which the
goods are laden, and everything being found on examination there to correspond, she shall be permitted to break bulk and land the said goods without being subject to the payment of any additional duty thereon.

But if on such examination the Superintendent of Customs shall detect
any fraud on the revenue in the case, then the goods shall be subject to forfeiture and confiscation to the Chinese Government.

Article XXI.

Subjects of China who may be guilty of any criminal act towards citizens of the United States shall be arrested and punished by the Chinese authorities according to the laws of China, and citizens of the United States
who may commit any crime in China shall be subject to be tried and punished only by the Consul or other public functionary of the United States

thereto authorized according to the laws of the United States; and in order
to the prevention of all controversy and disaffection, justice shall be
equitably and impartially administered on both sides.

Article XXII.

Relations of peace and amity between the United States and China being
established by this Treaty, and the vessels of the United States being admitted to trade freely to and from the five ports of China open to Foreign
commerce, it is further agreed that in case at any time hereafter China
should be at war with any Foreign nation whatever, and should for that
cause exclude such nation from entering her ports, still the vessels of the
United States shall not the less continue to pursue their commerce in free-
dom and security, and to transport goods to and from the ports of the bel-
ligerent parties, full respect being paid to the neutrality of the flag of the
United States: Provided that the said flag shall not protect vessels engaged
in the importation of officers or soldiers in the enemy's service, nor shall
said flag be fraudulently used to enable the enemy's ships with their car-
goes to enter the ports of China; but all such vessels so offending shall be
subject to forfeiture and confiscation to the Chinese Government.

Article XXIII.

The Consuls of the United States at each of the five ports open to Foreign trade shall make annually to the respective Governors-General thereof a detailed report of the number of vessels belonging to the United States
which have entered and left said ports during the year, and of the amount
and value of goods imported or exported in said vessels, for transmission
to and inspection of the Board of Revenue.

Article XXIV.

If citizens of the United States have special occasion to address any
communication to the Chinese local officers of Government, they shall submit the same to their Consul or other officer to determine if the language
be proper and respectful, and the matter just and right; in which event he
shall transmit the same to the appropriate authorities for their consideration and action in the premises. In like manner, if subjects of China have
special occasion to address the Consul of the United States, they shall submit the communication to the local authorities of their own Government to
determine if the language be respectful and proper, and the matter just and
right; in which case the said authorities will transmit the same to the Consul or other functionary for his consideration and action in the premises.
And if controversies arise between citizens of the United States and subjects
of China which cannot be amicably settled otherwise, the same shall be examined and decided conformably to justice and equity by the public officers

of the two nations acting in conjunction.

Article XXV.

All questions in regards to rights, whether of property or person, arising between citizens of the United States in China shall be subject to the jurisdiction of and regulated by the authorities of their own Government; and all controversies occurring in China between the citizens of the United States and the subjects of any other Government shall be regulated by the Treaties existing between the United States and such Governments respectively, without interference on the part of China.

Article XXVI.

Merchant vessels of the United States lying in the waters of the five ports of China open to Foreign commerce will be under the jurisdiction of the officers of their own Government, who, with the masters and owners thereof, will manage the same, without control on the part of China. For injuries done to the citizens or the commerce of the United States by any Foreign power, the Chinese Government will not hold itself bound to make reparation.

But if the merchant vessels of the United States, while within the waters over which the Chinese Government exercise jurisdiction, be plundered by robbers or pirates, then the Chinese local authorities, civil and military, on receiving information thereof, will arrest the said robbers or pirates and punish them according to law, and will cause all the property which can be recovered to be placed in the hands of the nearest Consul or other officer of the United States, to be by him restored to the true owner; but if, by reason of the extent of territory and numerous population of China, it should in any case happen that the robbers cannot be apprehended or the property only in part recovered, then the law will take its course in regard to the local authorities, but the Chinese Government will not make indemnity for the goods lost....

Done at Wanghia, this third day of July in the year of our Lord Jesus Christ one thousand eight hundred and forty-four, and of Taou-Kwang, the twenty-fourth year, fifth month, and eighteenth day.

(Signed) C. Cushing

(Signed)   Kiyeng

Document 16

ADDITIONAL ARTICLES TO THE TREATY BETWEEN
THE UNITED STATES OF AMERICA AND THE TA TSING EMPIRE
[CHINA] OF THE 18th OF JUNE, 1858.

Signed at Washington, 28th July, 1868.
Ratified at Peking, 23rd November, 1869.

Whereas, since the conclusion of the Treaty between the United States
of America and the Ta Tsing Empire (China) of the 18th of June, 1858, circumstances have arisen showing the necessity of additional articles thereto: the President of the United States and the August Sovereign of the Ta
Tsing Empire have named for their Plenipotentiaries to wit the President
of the United States of America, William H. Seward, Secretary of State;
and His Majesty the Emperor of China, Anson Burlingame, accredited as
his Envoy Extraordinary and Minister Plenipotentiary, and Chih Kang, and
Sun Chia-ku, of the second Chinese rank, associated high Envoys and Ministers of his said Majesty; and the said Plenipotentiaries, after having exchanged their full powers, found to be in due and proper form, have agreed
upon the following articles:--

Article I.

His Majesty the Emperor of China, being of the opinion that in making
concessions to the citizens or subjects of foreign powers, of the privilege
of residing on certain tracts of land, or resorting to certain waters of that
Empire, for purposes of trade, he has by no means relinquished his right
of eminent domain or dominion over the said lands and waters, hereby
agrees that no such concession or grant shall be construed to give to any
power or party, which may be at war with or hostile to the United States,
the right to attack the citizens of the United States, or their property, within the said lands or waters: And the United States, for themselves, hereby agree to abstain from offensively attacking the citizens or subjects of
any power or party or their property, with which they may be at war, on
any such tract of land or waters of the said Empire. But nothing in this
article shall be construed to prevent the United States from resisting an attack by any hostile power or party upon their citizens or their property.

It is further agreed that if any right or interest in any tract of land in
China has been, or shall hereafter be, granted by the Government of China
to the United States or their citizens for purposes of trade or commerce,--
that grant shall in no event be construed to divest the Chinese authorities
of their right of jurisdiction over persons and property within said tract of

land except so far as the right may have been expressly relinquished by Treaty.

Article II.

The United States of America and His Majesty the Emperor of China, believing that the safety and prosperity of commerce will thereby best be promoted, agree that any privilege or immunity in respect to trade or navigation within the Chinese dominions which may not have been stipulated for by Treaty, shall be subject to the discretion of the Chinese Government, and may be regulated by it accordingly, but not in a manner or spirit incompatible with the Treaty stipulation of the parties.

Article III.

The Emperor of China shall have the right to appoint Consuls at ports of the United States, who shall enjoy the same privileges and immunities as those which are enjoyed by public law and Treaty in the United States by the Consuls of Great Britain and Russia or either of them.

Article IV.

The 29th Article of the Treaty of the 18th of June, 1858, having stipulated for the exemption of Christian citizens of the United States and Chinese Converts from persecution in China on account of their faith; it is further agreed that citizens of the United States in China of every religious persuasion, and Chinese subjects in the United States, shall enjoy entire liberty of conscience, and shall be exempt from all disability or persecution on account of their religious faith or worship in either country. Cemeteries for sepulture of the dead, of whatever nativity or nationality, shall be held in respect and free from disturbance or profanation.

Article V.

The United States of America and the Emperor of China, cordially recognize the inherent and inalienable right of man to change his home and allegiance, and also the mutual advantage of the free migration and emigration of their citizens and subjects respectively from the one country to the other for the purposes of curiosity, of trade, or as permanent residents. The high Contracting Parties, therefore, join in reprobating any other than an entirely voluntary emigration for these purposes. They consequently agree to pass laws, making it a penal offense for a citizen of the United States, or a Chinese subject, to take Chinese subjects either to the United States or to any other foreign country; or for a Chinese subject or a citizen of the United States to take citizens of the United States to China, or to any other foreign country, without their free and voluntary consent respectively,

Article VI.

Citizens of the United States visiting or residing in China, shall enjoy the same privileges, immunities, or exemptions in respect to travel or residence as may there be enjoyed by the citizens or subjects of the most favoured nation. And, reciprocally, Chinese subjects visiting or residing in the United States, shall enjoy the same privileges, immunities, and exemptions in respect to travel or residence as may there be enjoyed by the citizens or subjects of the most favoured nation. But nothing herein contained shall be held to confer naturalization upon citizens of the United States in China, nor upon the subjects of China in the United States.

Article VII.

Citizens of the United States shall enjoy all the privileges of the public educational institutions under the control of the Government of China; and reciprocally, Chinese subjects shall enjoy all the privileges of the public educational institutions under the control of the Government of the United States, which are enjoyed in the respective countries by the citizens or subjects of the most favoured nation. The citizens of the United States may freely establish and maintain schools within the Empire of China at those places where foreigners are by Treaty permitted to reside; and reciprocally, the Chinese subjects may enjoy the same privileges and immunities in the United States.

Article VIII.

The United States, always disclaiming and discouraging all practices of unnecessary dictation and intervention by one nation in the affairs or domestic administration of another, do hereby freely disclaim and disavow any intention or right to intervene in the domestic administration of China in regard to the construction of railroads, telegraphs, or other material internal improvements. On the other hand, His Majesty the Emperor of China reserves to himself the right to decide the time and manner and circumstances of introducing such improvements within his dominions. With this mutual understanding it is agreed by the contracting parties that, if at any time hereafter, his Imperial Majesty shall determine to construct, or cause to be constructed, works of the character mentioned, within the Empire, and shall make application to the United States, or any other Western Power for facilities to carry out that policy, the United States will in that case designate or authorize suitable Engineers to be employed by the Chinese Government, and will recommend to other nations an equal compliance with such applications: the Chinese Government in that case protecting such Engineers in their persons and property, and paying them a reasonable compensation for their services.

In faith whereof, the respective Plenipotentiaries have signed this Treaty and thereto affixed the seals of their arms.

Done at Washington, the 28th day of July, in the year of Our Lord one thousand eight hundred and sixty-eight.

(Signed) William H. Seward

(Signed) Anson Burlingame

(Signed) Chih-Kang

(Signed) Sun Chia-Ku

Document 17

THE TREATY BETWEEN THE REPUBLIC OF CHINA AND
THE UNITED STATES OF AMERICA FOR THE RELINQUISHMENT
OF EXTRATERRITORIAL RIGHTS IN CHINA AND THE
REGULATION OF RELATED MATTERS.

Signed at Washington, January 11, 1943.
Ratifications exchanged at Washington, May 20, 1943.

The Republic of China and The United States of America, desirous of
emphasizing the friendly relations which have long prevailed between their
two peoples and of manifesting their common desire as equal and sovereign
States that the high principles in the regulation of human affairs to which
they are committed shall be made broadly effective, have resolved to con-
clude a treaty for the purpose of adjusting certain matters in the relations
of the two countries, and have appointed as their Plenipotentiaries:

The President of the National Government of the Republic of China,
    Dr. Wei Tao-ming, Ambassador Extraordinary and Plenipotentiary
of the Republic of China to the United States of America; and

The President of the United States of America,
    Mr. Cordell Hull, Secretary of State of the United States of America;

Who, having communicated to each other their full powers found to be
in due form, have agreed upon the following articles:

Article I.

All those provisions of treaties or agreements in force between the
United States of America and the Republic of China which authorize the
Government of the United States of America or its representatives to exercise jurisdiction over nationals of the United States of America in the territory of the Republic of China are hereby abrogated. Nationals of the
United States of America in such territory shall be subject to the jurisdiction of the Government of the Republic of China in accordance with the principles of international law and practice.

Article II.

The Government of the United States of America considers that the
Final Protocol concluded at Peking on September 7, 1901, between the Chinese Government and other governments, including the Government of the

United States of America, should be terminated and agrees that the rights accorded to the Government of the United States of America under that Protocol and under agreements supplementary thereto shall cease.

The Government of the United States of America will cooperate with the Government of the Republic of China for the reaching of any necessary agreements with other governments concerned for the transfer to the Government of the Republic of China of the administration and control of the Diplomatic Quarter at Peiping, including the official assets and the offical obligations of the Diplomatic Quarter, it being mutually understood that the Government of the Republic of China in taking over administration and control of the Diplomatic Quarter will make provision for the assumption and discharge of the official obligations and liabilities of the Diplomatic Quarter and for the recognition and protection of all legitimate rights therein.

The Government of the Republic of China hereby accords to the Government of the United States of America a continued right to use for official purposes the land which has been allocated to the Government of the United States of America in the Diplomatic Quarter in Peiping, on parts of which are located buildings belonging to the Government of the United States of America.

Article III.

The Government of the United States of America considers that the International Settlements at Shanghai and Amoy should revert to the administration and control of the Government of the Republic of China and agrees that the rights accorded to the Government of the United States of America in relation to those Settlements shall cease.

The Government of the United States of America will cooperate with the Government of the Republic of China for the reaching of any necessary agreements with other governments concerned for the transfer to the Government of the Republic of China of the administration and control of the International Settlements at Shanghai and Amoy, including the official assets and the official obligations of those Settlements, it being mutually understood that the Government of the Republic of China in taking over administration and control of those Settlements will make provision for the assumption and discharge of the official obligations and liabilities of those Settlements and for the recognition and protection of all legitimate rights therein.

Article IV.

In order to obviate any questions as to existing rights in respect of or as to existing titles to real property in territory of the Republic of China possessed by nationals (including corporations or associations), or by the Government, of the United States of America, particularly questions which

might arise from the abrogation of the provisions of treaties or agreements
as stipulated in Article 1, it is agreed that such existing rights or titles
shall be indefeasible and shall not be questioned upon any ground except upon proof, established through due process of law, of fraud or of fraudulent
or other dishonest practices in the acquisition of such rights or titles, it
being understood that no right or title shall be rendered invalid by virtue
of any subsequent change in the official procedure through which it was acquired. It is also agreed that these rights or titles shall be subject to the
laws and regulations of the Republic of China concerning taxation, national
defense, and the right of eminent domain, and that no such rights or titles
may be alienated to the government or nationals (including corporations or
associations) of any third country without the express consent of the Government of the Republic of China.

It is also agreed that if it should be the desire of the Government of the
Republic of China to replace, by new deeds of ownership, existing leases
in perpetuity or other documentary evidence relating to real property held
by nationals, or by the Government, of the United States of America, the
replacement shall be made by the Chinese authorities without charges of
any sort and the new deeds of ownership shall fully protect the holders of
such leases or other documentary evidence and their legal heirs and as-
signs without diminution of their prior rights and interests, including the
right of alienation.

It is further agreed that nationals or the Government of the United
States of America shall not be required or asked by the Chinese authorities
to make any payments of fees in connection with land transfers for or with
relation to any period prior to the effective date of this treaty.

Article V.

The Government of the United States of America having long accorded
rights to nationals of the Republic of China within the territory of the United
States of America to travel, reside and carry on trade throughout the whole
extent of that territory, the Government of the Republic of China agrees to
accord similar rights to nationals of the United States of America within
the territory of the Republic of China. Each of the two Governments will
endeavor to have accorded in territory under its jurisdiction to nationals of
the other country, in regard to all legal proceedings, and to matters relating to the administration of justice, and to the levying of taxes or requirements in connection therewith, treatment not less favorable than that accorded to its own nationals.

Article VI.

The Government of the United States of America and the Government
of the Republic of China mutually agree that the consular officers of each
country, duly provided with exequaturs, shall be permitted to reside in
such ports, places and cities as may be agreed upon. The consular officers
of each country shall have the right to interview, to communicate with, and
to advise nationals of their country within their consular districts; they

shall be informed immediately whenever nationals of their country are under detention or arrest or in prison or are awaiting trial in their consular districts and they shall, upon notification to the appropriate authorities, be permitted to visit any such nationals; and, in general, the consular officers of each country shall be accorded the rights, privileges, and immunities enjoyed by consular officers under modern international usage.

It is likewise agreed that the nationals of each country, in the territory of the other country, shall have the right at all times to communicate with the consular officers of their country. Communications to their consular officers from nationals of each country who are under detention or arrest or in prison or are awaiting trial in the territory of the other country shall be forwarded to such consular officers by the local authorities.

Article VII.

The Government of the United States of America and the Government of the Republic of China mutually agree that they will enter into negotiations for the conclusion of a comprehensive modern treaty of friendship, commerce, navigation and consular rights, upon the request of either Government or in any case within six months after the cessation of the hostilities in the war against the common enemies in which they are now engaged. The treaty to be thus negotiated will be based upon the principles of international law and practice as reflected in modern international procedures and in the modern treaties which the Government of the United States of America and the Government of the Republic of China respectively have in recent years concluded with other governments.

Pending the conclusion of a comprehensive treaty of the character referred to in the preceding paragraph, if any questions affecting the rights in territory of the Republic of China of nationals (including corporations or associations), or of the Government, of the United States of America should arise in future and if these questions are not covered by the present treaty, or by the provisions of existing treaties, conventions, or agreements between the Government of the United States of America and the Government of the Republic of China not abrogated by or inconsistent with this treaty, such questions shall be discussed by representatives of the two Governments and shall be decided in accordance with generally accepted principles of international law and with modern international practice.

Article VIII.

The present treaty shall come into force on the day of the exchange of ratifications.

The present treaty shall be ratified, and the ratifications shall be exchanged at Washington as soon as possible.

Signed and sealed in the Chinese and English languages, both equally authentic, in duplicate, at Washington, this eleventh day of the first month of the thirty-second year of the Republic of China, corresponding to January 11, 1943.

(Signed) Wei Tao-Ming

(Signed)   Cordell Hull

C. JUDICIAL DECISIONS

Document 18

THE PEOPLE, RESPONDENT, v. GEORGE W. HALL, APPELLANT.
Supreme Court of the State of California, 1854.

Mr. Ch. J. Murray delivered the opinion of the Court. Mr. J. Heyden-feldt concurred.

The appellant, a free white citizen of this State, was convicted of murder upon the testimony of Chinese witnesses.

The point involved in this case is the admissibility of such evidence.

The 394th section of the Act Concerning Civil Cases provides that no Indian or Negro shall be allowed to testify as a witness in any action or proceeding in which a white person is a party.

The 14th section of the Act of April 16th, 1850, regulating Criminal Proceedings, provides that "No black or mulatto person, or Indian, shall be allowed to give evidence in favor of, or against a white man."

The true point at which we are anxious to arrive is, the legal significa-tion of the words, "black, mulatto, Indian, and white person," and whether the Legislature adopted them as generic terms, or intended to limit their application to specific types of the human species. . . .

The Act of Congress, in defining what description of aliens may be-come naturalized citizens, provides that every "free white citizen," etc. . . .

If the term "white," as used in the Constitution, was not understood in its generic sense as including the Caucasian race, and necessarily exclud-ing all others, where was the necessity of providing for the admission of Indians to the privilege of voting, by special legislation?

We are of the opinion that the words "white," "Negro," "mulatto," "Indian," and "black person," wherever they occur in our Constitution and laws, must be taken in their generic sense, and that, even admitting the Indian of this continent is not of the Mongolian type, that the words "black person," in the 14th section, must be taken as contradistinguished from white, and necessarily excludes all races other than the Caucasian.

We have carefully considered all the consequences resulting from a different rule of construction, and are satisfied that even in a doubtful case, we would be impelled to this decision on ground of public policy.

The same rule which would admit them to testify, would admit them to all the equal rights of citizenship, and we might soon see them at the polls, in the jury box, upon the bench, and in our legislative halls.

This is not a speculation which exists in the excited and overheated imagination of the patriot and statesman, but it is an actual and present danger.

The anomalous spectacle of a distinct people, living in our community, recognizing no laws of this State, except through necessity, bringing with them their prejudices and national feuds, in which they indulge in open violation of law; whose mendacity is proverbial; a race of people whom nature has marked as inferior, and who are incapable of progress or intellectual development beyond a certain point, as their history has shown; differing in language, opinions, color, and physical conformation; between whom and ourselves nature has placed an impassable difference, is now presented, and for them is claimed, not only the right to swear away the life of a citizen, but the further privilege of participating with us in administering the affairs of our Government.

These facts were before the Legislature that framed this Act, and have been known as matters of public history to every subsequent Legislature.

There can be no doubt as to the intention of the Legislature, and that if it had ever been anticipated that this class of people were not embraced in the prohibition, then such specific words would have been employed as would have put the matter beyond any possible controversy.

For these reasons, we are of opinion that the testimony was inadmissible.

The judgment is reversed and the cause remanded.

Document 19

THE CHINESE EXCLUSION CASE:
CHAE CHAN PING v. UNITED STATES.
United States Supreme Court, 1889.

(Chae Chan Ping, the appellant, was a Chinese national residing in the United States from 1875 to 1887. Then he left for China with a return certificate. Upon his arrival in the Port of San Francisco a year later, he was prohibited from landing by the authorities concerned for the reason that his return certificate had become invalid as a result of a new Act passed by Congress on October 1, 1888. The lower court refused to release him from detention. The argument of the appellant was based on the ground that the new Act was in conflict with the existing treaty between the United States and China and the earlier statutes of the United States.)

MR. JUSTICE FIELD delivered the opinion of the court. . . .

There being nothing in the treaties between China and the United States to impair the validity of the act of Congress of October 1, 1888, was it on any other ground beyond the competency of Congress to pass it? If so, it must be because it was not within the power of Congress to prohibit Chinese laborers who had at the time departed from the United States, or should subsequently depart, from returning to the United States. Those laborers are not citizens of the United States; they are aliens. That the government of the United States through the action of the legislative department, can exclude aliens from its territory is a proposition which we do not think open to controversy. Jurisdiction over its own territory to that extent is an incident of every independent nation. It is a part of its independence. If it could not exclude aliens it would be to that extent subject to the control of another power. As said by this court in the case of The Exchange, 7 Cranch, 116, 136, speaking by Chief Justice Marshall: "The jurisdiction of the nation within its own territory is necessarily exclusive and absolute. It is susceptible of no limitation not imposed by itself. Any restriction upon it, deriving validity from an external source, would imply a diminution of its sovereignty to the extent of the restriction, and an investment of that sovereignty to the same extent in that power which could impose such restriction. All exceptions, therefore, to the full and complete power of a nation within its own territories, must be traced up to the consent of the nation itself. They can flow from no other legitimate source."

While under our Constitution and form of government the great mass of local matters is controlled by local authorities, the United States, in their relation to foreign countries and their subjects or citizens are one nation, invested with powers which belong to independent nations, the exercise of which can be invoked for the maintenance of its absolute independence and security throughout its entire territory. The powers to declare war, make treaties, suppress insurrection, repel invasion, regulate foreign commerce, secure republican governments to the States, and admit

subjects of other nations to citizenship, are all sovereign powers, restricted in their exercise only by the Constitution itself and considerations
of public policy and justice which control, more or less, the conduct of
all civilized nations. As said by this court in the case of Cohens v. Virginia, 6 Wheat. 264, 413, speaking by the same great Chief Justice: "That
the United States form, for many, and for most important purposes, a
single nation, has not yet been denied. In war, we are one people. In
making peace we are one people. In all commercial regulations, we are
one and the same people. In many other respects, the American people
are one; and the government which is alone capable of controlling and
managing their interests in all these respects, is the government of the
Union. It is their government, and in that character they have no other.
America has chosen to be in many respects, and to many purposes, a
nation; and for all these purposes her government is complete; to all
these objects, it is competent. The people have declared, that in the
exercise of all powers given for these objects, it is supreme. It can then
in effecting these objects legitimately control all individuals or governments within the American territory. The constitution and laws of a State,
so far as they are repugnant to the Constitution and laws of the United
States, are absolutely void. These States are constituent parts of the
United States. They are members of one great empire -- for some purposes sovereign, for some purpose subordinate." The same view is expressed in a different form by Mr. Justice Bradley, in Knox v. Lee, 12
Wall. 457, 555, where he observes that "the United States is not only
a government, but it is a national government, and the only government
in this country that has the character of nationality. It is invested with
power over all the foreign relations of the country, war, peace and negotiations and intercourse with other nations; all of which are forbidden
to the state governments." . . .

The control of local matters being left to local authorities, and
national matters being entrusted to the government of the Union, the problem of free institutions existing over a widely extended country, having
different climates and varied interests, has been happily solved. For
local interests the several States of the Union exist, but for national
purposes, embracing our relations with foreign nations, we are but one
people, one nation, one power.

To preserve its independence, and give security against foreign
aggression and encroachment, is the highest duty of every nation, and
to attain these ends nearly all other considerations are to be subordinated.
It matters not in what form such aggression and encroachment come,
whether from the foreign nation acting in its national character or from
vast hordes of its people crowding in upon us. The government possessing
the powers which are to be exercised for protection and security, is
clothed with authority to determine the occasion on which the powers shall
be called forth; and its determination, so far as the subjects affected are
concerned, are necessarily conclusive upon all its departments and officers.
If, therefore, the government of the United States, through its legislative
department, considers the presence of foreigners of a different race
in this country, who will not assimilate with us, to be dangerous to its
peace and security, their exclusion is not be be stayed because at the

time there are no actual hostilities with the nation of which the foreigners are subjects. The existence of war would render the necessity of the proceeding only more obvious and pressing. The same necessity, in a less pressing degree, may arise when war does not exist, and the same authority which adjudges the necessity in one case must also determine it in the other. In both cases its determination is conclusive upon the judiciary. If the government of the country of which the foreigners excluded are subjects is dissatisfied with this action it can make complaint to the executive head of our government, or resort to any other measure which, in its judgment, its interests or dignity may demand; and there lies its only remedy.

The power of the government to exclude foreigners from the country whenever, in its judgment, the public interests require such exclusion, has been asserted in repeated instances, and never denied by the executive or legislative departments. . . . In a dispatch to Mr. Fay, our minister to Switzerland, in March, 1856, Mr. Marcy, Secretary of State under President Pierce, writes: "Every society possesses the undoubted right to determine who shall compose its members, and it is exercised by all nations, both in peace and war." "It may always be questionable whether a resort to this power is warranted by the circumstances, or what department of the government is empowered to exert it; but there can be no doubt that it is possessed by all nations, and that each may decide for itself when the occasion arises demanding its exercise." In a communication in September, 1869, to Mr. Washburne, our minister to France, Mr. Fish, Secretary of State under President Grant, uses this language: "The control of the people within its limits, and the right to expel from its territory persons who are dangerous to the peace of the State, are too clearly within the essential attributes of sovereignty to be seriously contested. Strangers visiting or sojourning in a foreign country voluntarily submit themselves to its laws and customs, and the municipal laws of France, authorizing the expulsion of strangers, are not of such recent date, nor has the exercise of the power by the government of France been so infrequent, that sojourners within her territory can claim surprise when the power is put in force." In a communication to Mr. Foster, our minister to Mexico in July, 1879, Mr. Evarts, Secretary of State under President Hayes, referring to the power vested in the constitution of Mexico to expel objectionable foreigners, says: "The admission that, as that constitution now stands and is interpreted, foreigners who render themselves harmful or objectionable to the general government must expect to be liable to the exercise of the power adverted to, even in time of peace, remains, and no good reason is seen for departing from that conclusion now. But, while there may be no expedient basis on which to found objection, on principle and in advance of a special case thereunder, to the constitutional right thus asserted by Mexico, yet the manner of carrying out such asserted right may be highly objectionable. You would be fully justified in making earnest remonstrances should a citizen of the United States be expelled from Mexican territory without just steps to assure the grounds of such expulsion, and in bringing the fact to the immediate knowledge of the Department." In a communication to Mr. W. J. Stillman, under date of August 3, 1882, Mr. Frelinghuysen, Secretary of

State under President Arthur, writes: "This government cannot contest the right of foreign governments to exclude, on police or other grounds, American citizens from their shores." Wharton's International Law Digest, § 206.

The exclusion of paupers, criminals and persons afflicted with incurable diseases, for which statutes have been passed, is only an application of the same power to particular classes of persons, whose presence is deemed injurious or a source of danger to the country. As applied to them, there has never been any question as to the power to exclude them. The power is constantly exercised; its existence is involved in the right of self-preservation. . . .

The power of exclusion of foreigners being an incident of sovereignty belonging to the government of the United States, as a part of those sovereign powers delegated by the Constitution, the right to its exercise at any time when, in the judgment of the government, the interests of the country require it, cannot be granted away or restrained on behalf of any one. The powers of government are delegated in trust to the United States, and are incapable of transfer to any other parties. They cannot be abandoned or surrendered. Nor can their exercise be hampered, when needed for the public good, by any considerations of private interest. The exercise of these public trusts is not the subject of barter or contract. Whatever license, therefore, Chinese laborers may have obtained, previous to the act of October 1, 1888, to return to the United States after their departure, is held at the will of the government, revocable at any time, at its pleasure. Whether a proper consideration by our government of its previous laws, or a proper respect for the nation whose subjects are affected by its action, ought to have qualified its inhibition and made it applicable only to persons departing from the country after the passage of the act, are not questions for judicial determination. If there be any just ground of complaint on the part of China, it must be made to the political department of our government, which is alone competent to act upon the subject. . . .

Order affirmed.

Document 20

FONG YUE TING v. UNITED STATES.
United States Supreme Court, 1893.

Appeals from the Circuit Court of the United States for the Southern
District of New York.

These were three writs of habeas corpus, granted by the Circuit
Court of the United States for the Southern District of New York, upon
petitions of Chinese laborers, arrested and held (for deportation) by the
marshal of the district for not having certificates of residence, under
section 6 of the act of May 5, 1892, c. 60. . . .

The first petition alleged that the petitioner was a person of the
Chinese race, born in China, and not a naturalized citizen of the United
States; that in or before 1879 he came to the United States, with the intention of remaining and taking up his residence therein, and with no
definite intention of returning to China, and had ever since been a permanent resident of the United States, and for more than a year last past
had resided in the city, county and State of New York, and within the
second district for the collection of internal revenue in that State; that
he had not, since the passage of the act of 1892, applied to the collector
of internal revenue of that district for a certificate of residence, as required by section 6, and was and always had been without such certificate
of residence; and that he was arrested by the marshal, claiming authority
to do so under that section, without any writ or warrant. The return of
the marshal stated that the petitioner was found by him within the jurisdiction of the United States, and in the Southern District of New York,
without the certificate of residence required by that section; that he had
therefore arrested him with the purpose and intention of taking him before
a United States judge within that district; and that the petitioner admitted
to the marshal, in reply to questions put through an interpreter, that
he was a Chinese laborer, and was without the required certificate of
residence. . . .

In each case, the Circuit Court, after a hearing upon the writ of
habeas corpus and the return of the marshal, dismissed the writ of
habeas corpus, and allowed an appeal of the petitioner to this court,
and admitted him to bail pending the appeal. . . .

GRAY, J. The general principles of public law which lie at the
foundation of these cases are clearly established by previous judgments
of this court, and by the authorities therein referred to. . . .

Chinese laborers, therefore, like all other aliens residing in the
United States for a shorter or longer time, are entitled, so long as they
are permitted by the government of the United States to remain in the
country, to the safeguards of the Constitution, and to the protection of
the laws, in regard to their rights of person and of property, and to their
civil and criminal responsibility. But they continue to be aliens, having

taken no steps towards becoming citizens, and incapable of becoming such under the naturalization laws; and therefore remain subject to the power of Congress to expel them, or to order them to be removed and deported from the country, whenever in its judgment their removal is necessary or expedient for the public interest. . . .

Upon careful consideration of the subject, the only conclusion which appears to us to be consistent with the principles of international law, with the Constitution and the laws of the United States, and with the previous decisions of this court, is that in each of these cases the judgment of the Circuit Court, dismissing the writ of habeas corpus, is right and must be affirmed.

Document 21

UNITED STATES v. WONG KIM ARK
United States Supreme Court, 1898.

(Wong Kim Ark was born of Chinese parents in 1873, when they were domiciled residents in the United States. He went to China with his parents in 1890, but returned and was admitted as a citizen of the United States in the same year. In 1894, he made another trip to China. Upon his return to the United States the next year, he was denied re-admittance on the ground that as a Chinese laborer he was barred by the Chinese Exclusion Act.)

Mr. Justice Gray, after stating the case, delivered the opinion of the court.

The facts of this case, as agreed by the parties, are as follows: Wong Kim Ark was born in 1873 in the city of San Francisco, in the State of California and United States of America, and was and is a laborer. His father and mother were persons of Chinese descent, and subjects of the Emperor of China; they were at the time of his birth domiciled residents of the United States, having previously established and still enjoying permanent domicile and residence therein at San Francisco; they continued to reside and remain in the United States until 1890, when they departed for China; and during all the time of their residence in the United States they were engaged in business, and were never employed in any diplomatic or official capacity under the Emperor of China. Wong Kim Ark, ever since his birth, has had but one residence, to wit, in California, within the United States, and has there resided, claiming to be a citizen of the United States, and has never lost or changed that residence, or gained or acquired another residence; and neither he, nor his parents acting for him, ever renounced his allegiance to the United States, or did or committed any act or thing to exclude him therefrom. In 1890 (when he must have been about seventeen years of age) he departed for China on a temporary visit and with the intention of returning to the United States, and did return thereto by sea in the same year, and was permitted by the collector of customs to enter the United States, upon the sole ground that he was a native-born citizen of the United States. After such return, he remained in the United States, claiming to be a citizen thereof, until 1894, when he (being about twenty-one years of age, but whether a little above or a little under that age does not appear) again departed for China on a temporary visit and with the intention of returning to the United States; and he did return thereto by sea in August, 1895, and applied to the collector of customs for permission to land; and was denied such permission, upon the sole ground that he was not a citizen of the United States.

It is conceded that, if he is a citizen of the United States, the acts of Congress, known as the Chinese Exclusion Acts, prohibiting persons of the Chinese race, and especially Chinese laborers, from coming into the United States, do not and cannot apply to him.

The question presented by the record is whether a child born in the United States, of parents of Chinese descent, who, at the time of his birth, are subjects of the Emperor of China, but have permanent domicil and residence in the United States, and are there carrying on business, and are not employed in any diplomatic or official capacity under the Emperor of China, becomes at the time of his birth a citizen of the United States, by virtue of the first clause of the Fourteenth Amendment of the Constitution, "All persons born or naturalized in the United States, and subject to the jurisdiction thereof, are citizens of the United States and of the State wherein they reside." . . .

The evident intention, and the necessary effect, of the submission of this case to the decision of the court upon the facts agreed by the parties, were to present for determination the single question, stated at the beginning of this opinion, namely, whether a child born in the United States, of parents of Chinese descent, who, at the time of his birth, are subjects of the Emperor of China, but have a permanent domicile and residence in the United States, and are there carrying on business, and are not employed in any diplomatic or official capacity under the Emperor of China, becomes at the time of his birth a citizen of the United States. For the reason above stated, this court is of opinion that the question must be answered in the affirmative.

Order affirmed.

Mr. Chief Justice Fuller, with whom concurred Mr. Justice Harlan, dissenting. . . .

Document 22

WEEDIN, COMMISSIONER OF IMMIGRATION, v. CHIN BOW
United States Supreme Court, 1927.

Mr. Chief Justice Taft delivered the opinion of the court.

This is a writ of certiorari to review a judgment of the United States Circuit Court of Appeals for the Ninth Circuit, affirming an order of the District Court for the Western District of Washington allowing a writ of habeas corpus for Chin Bow, a Chinese boy ten years of age, and granting him a discharge. . . .

Chin Bow applied for admission to the United States at Seattle. The board of special inquiry of the Immigration Bureau at that place denied him admission on the ground that, though his father is a citizen, he is not a citizen, because at the time of his birth in China his father had never resided in the United States. Chin Bow was born March 29, 1914, in China. His father, Chin Dun was also born in China on March 8, 1894, and had never been in this country until July 18, 1922. Chin Dun was the son of Chin Tong, the respondent's grandfather. Chin Tong is forty-nine years old and was born in the United States.

The Secretary of Labor affirmed the decision of the board of inquiry, and the deportation of the respondent was ordered. He secured a writ of habeas corpus from the District Court. Upon a hearing, an order discharging him was entered without an opinion. On appeal by the United States, the Circuit Court of Appeals affirmed the judgement of the District Court, 7 F. (2d) 369, holding him to be a citizen under the provisions of §1993 of the Revised Statutes, which is as follows:

"All children heretofore born or hereafter born out of the limits and jurisdiction of the United States, whose fathers were or may be at the time of their birth citizens thereof, are declared to be citizens of the United States; but the rights of citizenship shall not descend to children whose fathers never resided in the United States."

The rights of Chin Bow are determined by the construction of this section. The Secretary of Labor, April 27, 1916, asked the opinion of Attorney General Gregory whether a rule of the Chinese regulations of his Department, which denied citizenship to foreign-born children of American Chinese, was a valid one. He advised that it was not, because §1993 applied to all children and therefore included Chinese children as well. The second question was whether foreign-born children of American-born Chinese fathers were entitled to enter the United States as citizens thereof, when they had continued to reside for some time in China after reaching their majorities, without any affirmative action on their part indicating an intention to remain citizens of the United States, and the Attorney General advised that they were, in spite of these circumstances, entitled to enter the United States as citizens thereof. 30 Op. A. G. 529.

The United States contends that the proviso of §1993, "but the rights of citizenship shall not descend to children whose fathers never resided in the United States," must be construed to mean that only the children whose fathers have resided in the United States before their birth become citizens under the section. It is claimed for the respondent that the residence of the father at any time in the United States before his death entitles his son whenever born to citizenship. These conflicting claims make the issue to be decided. . . .

It is very clear that the proviso in § 1993 has the same meaning as that which Congress intended to give it in the Act of 1790, except that it was then retrospective as it was in the Act of 1802, while in the Act of 1855 it was intended to be made prospective as well as retrospective. What was the source of the peculiar words of the proviso there seems to be no way of finding out, as the report of the discussion of the subject is not contained in any publication brought to our attention. It is evident, however, from the discussion in the First Congress, already referred to, that there was a strong feeling in favor of the encouragement of naturalization. There were some congressmen, although they did not prevail, who were in favor of naturalization by the mere application and taking of the oath. The time required for residence to obtain naturalization was finally limited to two years. In the Act of 1795 this was increased to five years, with three years for declaration of intention. Congress must have thought that the questions of naturalization and of the conferring of citizenship on sons of American citizens born abroad were related. . . .

Only two constructions seem to us possible, and we must adopt one or the other. The one is that the descent of citizenship shall be regarded as taking place at the birth of the person to whom it is to be transmitted, and that the words, "have never been resident in the United States," refer in point of time to the birth of the person to whom the citizenship is to descend. This is the adoption of the rule of jus sanguinis in respect to citizenship, and that emphasizes the fact and time of birth as the basis of it. We think the words, "the right of citizenship shall not descend to persons whose fathers have never been resident in the United States," are equivalent to saying that fathers may not have the power of transmitting by descent the right of citizenship until they shall become residents in the United States. The other view is that the words, "have never been resident in the United States," have reference to the whole life of the father until his death, and therefore that grandchildren of native-born citizens, even after they, having been born abroad, have lived abroad to middle age and without residing at all in the United States, will become citizens, if their fathers born abroad and living until old age abroad shall adopt a residence in the United States just before death. We are thus to have two generations of citizens who have been born abroad, lived abroad, the first coming to old age, and the second to maturity, and bringing up of a family without any relation to the United States at all until the father shall in his last days adopt a new residence. We do not think that such a construction accords with the probable attitude of Congress at the time of the adoption of this proviso into the statute. Its construction extends citizenship to a generation whose birth, minority, and majority, whose education, and whose family life have all been out of the United States and naturally within the civilization and environment of an alien country. The beneficiaries would have evaded the duties and responsibilities of American citizenship. They might be persons likely to become public charges or afflicted with disease; yet they would be entitled to enter as citizens of the United States. Van Dyne, Citizenship of the United States, p. 34.

As between the two interpretations, we feel confident that the first one was more in accord with the views of the First Congress. . . .

The expression, "the rights of citizenship shall descend," cannot refer to the time of the death of the father, because that is hardly the time when they do descend. The phrase is borrowed from the law of property. The descent of property comes only after the death of the ancestor. The transmission of right of citizenship is not at the death of the ancestor but at the birth of the child, and it seems to us more natural to infer that the conditions of the descent contained in the limiting proviso, so far as the father is concerned, must be perfected and have been performed at that time.

This leads to a reversal of the judgement of the Circuit Court of Appeals and a remanding of the respondent.

Reversed.

PART III

BIBLIOGRAPHY

PART III. BIBLIOGRAPHY

This selected bibliography consists of both primary and secondary sources concerning the immigration and status of the Chinese in the United States. Among government publications, the most important are Congressional Record, hearings, reports, and documents, particularly from the 1860's to 1943 prior to the repeal of the Chinese exclusion acts. Due to limitation of space, materials on immigration and naturalization in general for the postwar period are not included except those which bear special significance to the Chinese. Congressional acts and judicial decisions on Chinese immigration can be found in United States Statutes at Large and United States Supreme Court Reports and other federal and state reports, respectively. For convenient reference, all items under this category are arranged in alphabetical order of their titles.

Books occupy a large portion of the secondary sources; a small number of articles appearing in both official and unofficial publications are also selected. While major periodicals well known to the public only infrequently deal with the present subject, much information and viewpoints can be found in some specialized magazines, including the Amerasia Journal (quarterly, New Haven & Los Angeles), Bridge Magazine (bimonthly, New York), The Bridge (monthly, in Chinese, New York), Chinese-American Times (monthly, New York), Chinese Awareness (monthly, Los Angeles), and East/West, The Chinese-American Journal (Weekly, San Francisco). Most materials listed below are devoted to prewar discrimination against Chinese immigration, which is no longer a current issue for serious discussion since the repeal of all Chinese exclusion laws in 1943. Many Chinese dailies mentioned in the chronology have valuable and up to date reports.

In listing both official and unofficial materials, due attention is paid to their availability to the general public and the nature of this book. The selection is bound to be somewhat arbitrary, thus inevitably leaving out certain items of equal importance and value. Additional sources can be found in several bibliographies, including the following:

Appleton P. Clark Griffin, Select List of References on Chinese Immigration (Washington, D.C., 1904);

Robert Ernest Cowan and Boutwell Dunlop, Bibliography of the Chinese Question in the United States (San Francisco, 1909);

Isao Fujimoto, Michiyo Swift, and Rosalie Zucker, Asians in America: A Selected Annotated Bibliography (Davis, California, 1971);

William Wong Lum, Asians in America: A Bibliography and its two Supplements (Davis, California, 1969-1970).

For unpublished scholarly works on the subject, reference may be made to Lum's Asians in America: A Bibliography of Master's Theses and Doctoral Dissertations (Davis, California, 1970). Readers are also advised to consult the "Bibliography of Asian Studies," published annually as an extra issue of The Journal of Asian Studies (Ann Arbor, Michigan).

A. OFFICIAL PUBLICATIONS AND MATERIALS

Annual Reports of Immigration and Naturalization Service (under different
   titles and jurisdiction in the past), 1897-1971.

"Arrivals and Departures, San Francisco, Statistics of." Senate Misc.
   Doc. 90, 50th Cong., 1st Sess., 1887-1888.

"Asiatic Coolie Trade, Correspondence on." House Executive Doc. 16,
   37th Cong., 2nd Sess., 1861-1862.

"Burlingame Treaty, Resolutions of California Legislature on." House Misc.
   Doc. 120, 42nd Cong., 2nd Sess., 1871-1872.

"California Anti-Chinese Convention, 1886, Memorial of." Senate Misc.
   Doc. 107, 49th Cong., 1st Sess., 1885-1886.

California Legislature, Chinese Immigration. Sacramento, California:
   State Printing Office, 1887.

California Senate Reports of 1876 and 1878 on Chinese Immigration.

Census of Population, 1860-1970 (once every ten years).

"Chinese, Alleged Illegal Entry of." Senate Doc. 120, 55th Cong., 1st
   Sess., 1897.

"Chinese, Arrivals of." Senate Executive Doc. 97, 51st Cong., 1st Sess.,
   1889-1890.

"Chinese, Enumeration of." House Report 486, 51st Cong., 1st Sess.,
   1889-1890.

"Chinese, Exclusion of." Minority Report, House Report 407, 52nd Cong.,
   1st. Sess., 1891-1892.

"Chinese, Fraudulent Importation of." Senate Executive Doc., 103, 49th
   Cong., 1st Sess., 1885-1886.

"Chinese, Joint Special Committee on." Senate Report 689, 44th Cong.,
   2nd Sess., 1876-1877.

"Chinese, To Prevent Smuggling of." House Report 2503, 56th Cong., 2nd
   Sess., 1900-1901.

"Chinese Coolie Trade, Correspondence on." House Executive Doc. 88,

36th Cong., 1st Sess., 1859-1860.

"Chinese Exclusion." House Report 1231, 57th Cong., 1st Sess., 1901-1902.

"Chinese Exclusion: Hearings before the Committee on Immigration."
Senate Doc. 776, 57th Cong., 1st Sess., 1901-1902.

"Chinese Exclusion, Laws, etc. Relating to." Senate Doc. 291, 57th Cong.,
1st Sess., 1901-1902.

"Chinese Exclusion, Regulations Relating to." Senate Doc. 300, 57th Cong.,
1st. Sess., 1901-1902.

"Chinese Exclusion, Some Reasons for." Senate Doc. 137, 57th Cong.,
1st. Sess., 1901-1902.

"Chinese Exclusion, Wu Ting-fang on." Senate Doc. 162 and 164, 57th
Cong., 1st Sess., 1901-1902.

"Chinese Exclusion Acts, Repeal of the." Hearings before the House Committee on Immigration and Naturalization, May 19, 20, 26, 27, June 2, 3,
78th Cong., 1st Sess., 1943.

"Chinese Exclusion Law, Cost of Enforcing." Senate Executive Doc. 13,
53rd Cong., 1st Sess., 1893.

"Chinese Exclusion Law, For the Re-enactment of the; California Memorial." Senate Doc. 191, 57th Cong., 1st Sess., 1901-1902.

"Chinese Exclusion Law, Need of Amending." House Report 70, 53rd
Cong., 1st Sess., 1893.

"Chinese Exclusion Laws, Enforcement of." House Doc. 847, 59th Cong.,
1st   Sess., 1905-1906.

"Chinese Exclusion Laws, Repealing the." House Report 732, 78th Cong.,
1st Sess., 1943.

"Chinese for Omaha Exposition." House Doc. 68, 55th Cong., 1st Sess.,
1897.

"Chinese Immigration." House Report 240, 45th Cong., 2nd Sess., 1877-
1878; House Reports 62, 111, 45th Cong., 3rd Sess., 1878-1879; House
Reports 67, 1017, 47th Cong., 1st Sess., 1881-1882.

"Chinese Immigration, Depression in Business and." House Misc. Doc. 5,
46th Cong., 2nd Sess., 1879-1880.

"Chinese Immigration, Diplomatic Correspondence on." House Executive Doc. 70, 46th Cong., 2nd Sess., 1879-1880.

"Chinese Immigration, Resolution of California Legislature on." House Misc. Doc. 204, 43rd Cong., 1st Sess., 1873-1874.

"Chinese Immigration, Restriction of." House Report 2915, 51st Cong., 1st. Sess., 1889-1890.

"Chinese Immigration Bill, Veto of." House Executive Doc. 102, 45th Cong., 3rd Sess., 1878-1879.

"Chinese Immigration into Hawaii, Relative to." Hearings before the House Committee on Immigration and Naturalization, January 17, 1918, 65th Cong., 2nd Sess., 1918.

"Chinese in Transit." Senate Executive Doc. 106, 51st Cong., 1st Sess., 1889-1890.

"Chinese Laborers, Exclusion of." Senate Doc. 304, 57th Cong., 1st Sess., 1901-1902.

"Chinese Laborers, Pennsylvania Petition against." House Misc. Doc. 81, 42nd Cong., 3rd Sess., 1872-1873.

"Chinese on American Vessels." Senate Docs. 254, 281, 57th Cong., 1st Sess., 1901-1902.

"Chinese Refugees, Inquiry into Activities of Charles F. Hille with Relation to Certain." Hearings before the House Subcommittee on Immigration and Naturalization, January 24, 1922, 67th Cong., 1st Sess., 1921-1922.

"Chinese Refugees, Registration of." Hearings before the House Committee on Immigration and Naturalization, November 8, 1921, 67th Cong., 1st. Sess., 1921-1922.

"Chinese Registration." House Executive Doc. 152, 53rd Cong., 2nd Sess., 1893-1894.

"Chinese Registration, in Relation to." House Report 2043, 49th Cong., 1st Sess., 1885-1886.

"Chinese Wives of Certain American Citizens, To Admit to United States." House Report 1565, 71st Cong., 2nd Sess., 1929-1930.

Department of State Hearings before the Subcommittee of the Committee on Appropriations (House of Representatives, 85th Cong., 2nd Sess.).

Washington, D.C.: U.S. Government Printing Office, 1958.

Directory of Chinese Members of American College and University Faculties, 1959-1960. Washington, D.C.: Embassy of the Republic of China,
Office of the Cultural Counselor, 1960.

"Displaced Persons Act of 1948, Amending." House Report 2187, 81st
Cong., 2nd Sess., 1950.

"Entry of Certain Relatives of U.S. Citizens and Lawfully Resident Aliens,
Providing for." House Report 582, 86th Cong., 1st Sess., 1959.

"Exclusion, Arguments against." Senate Doc. 106, 57th Cong., 1st Sess.,
1901-1902.

"Exclusion Law, Amendment of." House Doc. 372, 54th Cong., 1st Sess.,
1895-1896.

"Exclusion Law, Appropriation for Enforcement of." Senate Executive
Doc. 111, 53rd Cong., 2nd Sess., 1893-1894.

"Exclusion Laws, Execution of." Senate Executive Doc. 41, 51st Cong.,
1st Sess., 1889-1890; House Executive Doc. 244, 52nd Cong., 1st Sess.,
1891-1892.

"Exclusion Laws, To Strengthen." House Docs. 471 and 472, 56th Cong.,
2nd Sess., 1900-1901.

"Exclusion of Japanese and Chinese, Petition for." Senate Doc. 292, 57th
Cong., 1st Sess., 1901-1902.

"Geary Law, Enforcement of." House Executive Docs. 9 and 10, 53rd
Cong., 1st Sess., 1893.

"Immigration, Restriction of." House Report 350, 68th Cong., 1st Sess.,
1924.

"Immigration and Nationality Act of June 27, 1952, and Its Amendments."
House Report, 1365, Senate Report 1137, 82nd Cong., 2nd Sess., 1952;
Senate Report 1057, 85th Cong., 1st Sess., 1957; House Report 13451,
85th Cong., 2nd Sess., 1958; House Reports 291, 398, Senate Report
475, 86th Cong., 1st Sess., 1959.

"Immigration and Nationality Act of October 3, 1965, and Its Amendments."
Public Law 91-136, 91st Cong., H.R. 3666, December 5, 1969; Public
Law 91-225, 91st Cong., S. 2593, April 7, 1970; Public Law 91-313, 91st

Cong., H.R. 14118, July 10, 1970; Pubic Law 92-584, 92nd Cong., H.R. 8273, October 27, 1972.

Immigration and Nationality Act, with Amendments and Notes on Related Laws and Summaries of Pertinent Judicial Decisions (6th Ed., revised through May 1, 1969). Washington, D.C.: U.S. Government Printing Office, 1969.

"Immigration and Naturalization Systems of the United States, The." Senate Report 1515, 81st Cong., 2nd Sess., 1950.

"Immigration Laws to Hawaiian Islands, Extension of." Senate Report 1654, 55th Cong., 3rd Sess., 1898-1899.

"Immigration Quotas Available to Asian and Pacific Peoples, To Make." House Report 65, 81st Cong., 1st Sess., 1949.

"Instruction to United States Minister in China." Senate Executive Doc. 175, 47th Cong., 1st Sess., 1881-1882.

Municipal Reports of the San Francisco Board of Supervisors (particularly the "Report of the Special Committee," 1884-1885).

"New Exclusion Legislation, Need of." House Report 255, 52nd Cong., 1st. Sess., 1891-1892.

"Oriental Race, Wives of American Citizens of." Hearings before the House Committee on Immigration and Naturalization, February 7, 1928, 70th Cong., 1st Sess., 1928.

"Oriental Veterans in Armed Forces of United States during the World War to Apply for Citizenship, To Permit Certain Resident." House Report 7170, 74th Cong., 1st Sess., 1935.

Overseas Chinese Yearbook, 1958. Taipei, Taiwan: Overseas Chinese Affairs Commission, 1959.

"Refuge Relief Act of 1953 and Its Amendments." House Report 1069, 83rd Cong., 1st Sess., 1953; Senate Report 2045, House Report 1323, 83rd Cong., 2nd Sess., 1954.

Report of the Immigration Commission (in 41 vols., with first 2 as abstract). Washington, D.C.: Immigration and Naturalization Service, 1911.

Statistical Abstract of the United States (Annual, 1879-1972). Washington,

D.C.: U.S. Bureau of the Census.

Treaty, Laws and Regulations Governing the Admission of Chinese. Washington, D.C.: Department of Commerce and Labor, Bureau of Immigration and Naturalization, 1911.

Vital Statistics of the United States, 1937-1958. Washington, D.C.: U.S. National Office of Vital Statistics.

B. BOOKS, PAMPHLETS, AND ARTICLES

Abbott, Edith, Historical Aspects of the Immigration Problem: Select Documents. Chicago: University of Chicago Press, 1926.

Adamic, Louis, Laughing in the Jungle. New York: Harper Brothers, 1932.

Adamic, Louis, The Native's Return. New York: Harper Brothers, 1934.

Adams, Romanzo, Interracial Marriages in Hawaii. New York: Macmillan Company, 1937.

Adams, Romanzo, The Peoples of Hawaii. New York: Institute of Pacific Relations, 1933.

Allport, Gordon W., The Nature of Prejudice. Reading, Mass: Addison-Wesley Publishing Co., 1954.

Auerbach, Frank, Immigration Laws of the United States. Indianapolis: Bobbs-Merrill Co., 1955; Supplement, 1958.

Ayscough, Florence, Chinese Women, Yesterday and Today. Boston: Houghton Mifflin Co., 1937.

Bancroft, Hubert Howe, History of California (The Works of Hubert Howe Bancroft, Vols. XVIII-XXIV), 7 vols. San Francisco: The History Co., and A. L. Bancroft Co., 1883-1890.

Barron, Milton L., People Who Intermarry. Syracuse, N.Y.: Syracuse University Press, 1946.

Barth, Gunther, Bitter Strength: A History of the Chinese in the United States, 1850-1870. Cambridge: Harvard University Press, 1964.

Beach, Walter G., Oriental Crime in California. Stanford: Stanford University Press, 1932.

Beck, Louis Joseph, New York's Chinatown. New York: Bohemia Publishing Co., 1898.

Bennett, Marion, American Immigration Policies--A History. Washington, D.C.: Public Affairs Press, 1963.

Berdahl, Clarence A., "The President's Veto of Private Bills," Political Science Quarterly, LII, No. 4 (December, 1937), pp. 505-531.

Bernard, William S. (ed.), American Immigration Policy: A Reappraisal. New York: Harper & Brothers, 1950.

Borgadus, E.S., Immigration and Race Attitudes. Boston: D.C. Heath & Co., 1928.

Bowers, D.F. (ed.), Foreign Influences in American Life. Princeton: Princeton University Press, 1944.

Boxer, C.R., "Notes on the Chinese Abroad in the Late Ming and Early Manchu Periods Compiled from Contemporary European Sources (1500-1750)," Tien Hsia Monthly, IX, No. 5 (August-December, 1939), pp. 447-468.

Briscoe, Edward Eugene, "Pershing's Chinese Refugees in Texas," The Southwestern Historical Quarterly, LXII, No. 4 (April, 1959), pp. 467-488.

Bromley, Isaac Hill, The Chinese Massacre at Rock Springs, Wyoming Territory, September 2, 1885. Boston: Franklin Press, Rand, Avery & Co., 1886.

Brown, F.J., and J.S. Roucek (eds.), One America: The History, Contributions, and Present Problems of Our Racial and National Minorities (3rd ed.). Englewood Cliffs, N.J.: Prentice-Hall, 1952.

Bruce, J. Campbell, The Golden Door. New York: Random House, 1954.

Buck, Pearl S., Of Men and Women. New York: John Day, 1941.

Burma, John H., "Research Note on the Measurement of Inter-Racial Marriage," American Journal of Sociology, XLVII, No. 6 (March, 1952), pp. 587-589.

Burrows, Edwin G., Hawaiian Americans. New Haven: Yale University

Press, 1940.

Campbell, Persia Crawford, Chinese Coolie Emigration to Countries Within the British Empire. London: P.S. King & Son, 1923.

Carter, Hugh, "Reappraising Our Immigration Policy," The Annals of the American Academy of Political and Social Science. CCLXII (March, 1949), pp. 1-192.

Cattell, Stuart H., Health, Welfare, and Social Organizations in Chinatown, New York City. New York: Community Service Society, 1962.

Cayton, Horace R., and Anne O. Lively, The Chinese in the United States and the Chinese Christian Churches. New York: National Council of the Churches of Christ in the United States of America, 1955.

Chang, Francis, "An Accomodation Program for Second Generation Chinese," Sociology and Social Research, XVIII (July-August, 1934), pp. 541-583.

Char, Tin-yuke, "Immigrant Chinese Societies in Hawaii," 61st Annual Report of the Hawaiian Historical Society (Honolulu: Advertising Co., 1953), pp. 29-32.

Chen, Ju-chou, Handbook of Chinese in America (in Chinese). New York, 1946.

Chen, K.F., "Overseas Chinese in the United States," Far Eastern Economic Review, 25 (July, 1958), pp. 142-144.

Chen, Lee-tai, Chung Kuo Hai Hwai Yee Ming Sze (The History of Chinese Immigration). Shanghai: Chung Hwa Press, 1946.

Chen, Ta., Chinese Migrations with Special Reference to Labor Conditions (Bulletin of the United States Bureau of Labor Statistics, No. 340). Washington, D.C.: U.S. Government Printing Office, 1923.

Chen, Ta, Emigrant Communities in South China. New York: Institute of Pacific Relations, 1940.

Ch'en, T'ien-ên (ed.), Welcome to Chinatown. New York: Henin, 1964.

Chinese Chamber of Commerce of New York, Inc., Fiftieth Anniversary. New York, 1957.

Chinese Chamber of Commerce of San Francisco, San Francisco Chinatown on Parade in Picture and Story. San Francisco, 1961.

Chinese Students in the United States, 1948-1955. New York: Committee on Educational Interchange Policy, 1956.

Chinese-American Restaurant Association of Greater New York, Inc., Twenty-seventh Anniversary. New York, 1960.

Chinn, Thomas W. (ed.), A History of the Chinese in California: A Syllabus. San Francisco: Chinese Historical Society of America, 1969.

Chiu, Ping, Chinese Labor in California. Madison: University of Wisconsin Press, 1963.

Chu, Daniel, and Samuel Chu, Passage to the Golden Gate. Garden City, N.Y.: Doubleday, 1967.

Chu, Jennings Pinkwei, Chinese Students in America: Qualities Associated with Their Success. New York: Columbia University Press, 1922.

Clappe, Louise, The Shirley Letters from the California Mines. New York: Alfred A. Knopf, 1961.

Clark, J.P., Deportation of Aliens from the United States. New York: Columbia University Press, 1931.

Coleman, Elizabeth, Chinatown, USA. New York: John Day, 1946.

Coman, Katherine, The History of Contract Labor in the Hawaiian Islands (Publication of the American Economic Association, 3rd series, Vol. IV, No. 3). New York: Macmillan Co., 1903.

Commager, Henry, Steele, Documents of American History. New York: F. S. Crofts & Co., 1940.

Commons, John R., Races and Immigrants in America. New York: Macmillan Co., 1924.

Condit, Ira M., The Chinaman As We See Him. Chicago: F.H. Revell Co., 1900.

"Congress Enacts Bill Benefiting Certain Relatives of United States Citizens and Lawful Resident Aliens," Interpreter Releases, XXXVI, No. 32 (September 21, 1959), pp. 235-243.

Coolidge, Mary Roberts, Chinese Immigration. New York: Henry Holt, 1909; Arno Press, 1969.

Coolidge, Mary Roberts, "Chinese Labor Competition on the Pacific Coast," The Annals of the American Academy of Political and Social Science, 34 (September, 1909), pp. 120-121.

Corbally, John, "Orientals in Seattle Schools," Sociology and Social Research, XVI (September-October, 1931), pp. 61-67.

Cornwell, Russell H., Why and How. Why the Chinese Emigrate, and the Means They Adopt for the Purpose of Reaching America, with Sketches of Travels, Amusing Incidents, Social Customs, etc. Boston: Lee & Shephard, 1871.

Culin, Stewart, "Customs of the Chinese in America," Journal of American Folklore, III, No. 10 (1890), pp. 347-352.

Daniels, Roger, The Politics of Prejudice. Gloucester, Mass.: Peter Smith, 1966.

Daniels, Roger, and Harry H. L. Kitano, American Racism: Exploration of the Nature of Prejudice. Englewood Cliffs, N.J.: Prentice-Hall, 1970.

Davie, Maurice R., World Immigration: With Special Reference to the United States. New York: Macmillan Co., 1936.

Davie, Maurice R., et al., Refugees in America. New York: Harper & Brothers, 1947.

Dennett, Tyler, "Seward's Far Eastern Policy," American Historical Review, XXVIII, No. 1 (October, 1922), pp. 45-62.

"Deportation Proceedings Decided by the Board August 2, 1955," Interpreter Releases, XXXIII, No. 38 (September 28, 1956), pp. 324-325.

Dillon, Richard H., The Hatchet Men: The Story of the Tong Wars in San Francisco's Chinatown. New York: Coward McCann, 1962.

Directory of Chinese Members of American College and University Faculties, 1956-1957. New York: Chinese Advisory Committee on Cultural Relations in America, 1957.

Divine, Robert A., American Immigration Policy, 1924-1952. New Haven: Yale University Press, 1957.

Dobie, Charles C., San Francisco's Chinatown. New York: Appleton-Century, 1936.

Dorland, C.P., "Chinese Massacre at Los Angeles in 1871," Annual Publications, Historical Society of Southern California, III, Pt. II (1894), pp. 22-26.

Dressler, Albert (ed.), California Chinese Chatter. San Francisco: A. Dressler, 1927.

Dulles, Foster R., China and America--Foreign Relations Since 1784. Princeton: Princeton University Press, 1946.

Duncan, H.G., Immigration and Assimilation. Boston: D.C. Heath & Co., 1933.

Dunning, William, Reconstruction, Political and Economic, 1865-1877. New York: Harper & Brothers, 1907.

Eaton, A.H., Immigrant Gifts to American Life. New York: Russell Sage Foundation, 1932.

Eaves, Lucile, A History of California Labor Legislation. Berkeley: University of California Press, 1910.

Eberhard, Wolfram, Chinese Festivals. New York: Henry Schuman, 1952.

Ecclesine, Margaret, "The Church in Chinatown, U.S.A.," Catholic Digest, August, 1960, pp. 57-62.

Elegant, Robert S., The Dragon's Seed: Peking and the Overseas Chinese. New York: St. Martin's Press, 1959.

Ellenwood, James Lee, One Generation after Another. New York: Charles Scribner & Sons, 1953.

Elstob, Winston, Chinatown, A Legend of Old Channery Row. Orinda, Calif.: Gondor's Sky Press, 1965.

Ennis, Edward J., "Some Current Problems in the Administration of Immigration Laws," Interpreter Releases, XXXII, No. 49 (December 12, 1955), pp. 379-385.

Fairchild, Henry Pratt, Immigration, A World Movement and Its American Significance (rev. ed.). New York: Macmillan Co., 1933.

Fairchild, Henry Pratt, The Melting-Pot Mistake. Boston: Little, Brown & Co., 1926.

Fairchild, Henry Pratt, Race and Nationality as Factors in American Life. New York: Ronald Press, 1947.

Farwell, Willard B., The Chinese at Home and Abroad. San Francisco: Bancroft, 1885; new ed., 1970.

Feldman, Herman, Racial Factors in American Industry. New York: Harper & Brothers, 1931.

Feng, Tzu-yu, Hua Ch'iao Ke Ming K'ai Kuo Shih (A History of Overseas Chinese Contributions to the Chinese Revolution). Taipei, Taiwan: Commercial Press, 1953.

Fields, Harold, The Refugee in the United States. New York: Oxford University Press, 1938.

Fisk University, Social Science Institute, Orientals and Their Cultural Adjustment. Nashville, Tenn: Fisk University, 1946.

Fitzgerald, Stephen, China and the Overseas Chinese: A Study of Peking's Changing Policy, 1949-1970. Cambridge, England: Cambridge University Press, 1972.

Foster, J. W., "The Chinese Boycott," Atlantic Monthly, 97 (January, 1906), pp. 118-127.

Frazier, E. Franklin, Race and Culture Contacts in the Modern World. New York: A. Knopf, 1957.

Freire, Paulo, Pedagogy of the Oppressed. New York: Herder & Herder, 1971.

Fried, Morton H. (ed.), Colloquium on Overseas Chinese. New York: Institute of Pacific Relations, 1958.

Galloway, George B., "Reform of Private Bill Procedure," Congressional Record (Appendix, May 12, 1949), pp. A2901-A2902.

Galloway, J.D., The First Transcontinental Railroad -- Central Pacific and Union Pacific. New York: Simmons-Boardman, 1950.

Garis, Roy L., Immigration Restriction. New York: Macmillan Co., 1928.

Gibson, Otis, The Chinese in America. Cincinnati: Hitchcock & Walden, 1877.

Gibson, William M., Aliens and the Law. Chapel Hill: University of North Carolina Press, 1940.

Gittler, Joseph, Understanding Minority Groups. New York: John Wiley & Sons, 1955.

Glazer, Nathan, and Davis McEntire (eds.), Housing and Minority Groups. Berkeley: University of California Press, 1960.

Glick, Clarence, "The Relation between Position and Status in the Assimilation of Chinese in Hawaii," American Journal of Sociology, XLVII, No. 5 (March, 1942), pp. 667-679.

Glick, Clarence, "Transition from Familism to Nationalism among Chinese in Hawaii," American Journal of Sociology, XLIII, No. 5 (March, 1938), pp. 734-743.

Gong, Eddie, "I Want to Marry An American Girl," The American Magazine, CLX, No. 3 (September, 1955), pp. 15-17, 82-85.

Gordon, Charles, and Harry N. Rosenfield, Immigration Law and Procedure. Albany: Banks & Co., 1959.

Graham, Virginia Taylor, "The Intelligence of Chinese Children in San Francisco," Journal of Comparative Psychology, VI, No. 1 (February, 1926), pp. 43-71.

Guilford, J.P., "Racial Preferences of A Thousand American University Students," Journal of Social Psychology, II, No. 2 (May, 1931), pp. 179-204.

Gulick, Sidney L., American Democracy and Asiatic Citizenship. New York: Charles Scribner & Sons, 1918.

Handlin, Oscar, Immigration as a Factor in American History. Englewood Cliffs, N.J.: Prentice-Hall, 1959.

Handlin, Oscar, The Newcomers: Negroes and Puerto Ricans in a Changing Metropolis. Garden City, N.Y.: Doubleday Anchor Books, 1962.

Handlin, Oscar, Race and Nationality in American Life. Boston: Little, Brown & Co., 1957.

Handlin, Oscar, This Was America. Cambridge: Harvard University Press, 1949.

Handlin, Oscar, Uprooted: The Epic Story of the Great Migrations That Made the American People. Boston: Little, Brown & Co., 1951.

Hankins, Frank, The Racial Basis of Civilization. New York: Alfred A. Knopf, 1926.

Hansen, Gladys C. (ed.), The Chinese in California (Selected by G. C. Hansen, annotated by W. F. Heintz). Portland, Oregon: R. Abel, 1970.

Hansen, Marcus Lee, The Atlantic Migration, 1607-1860. Cambridge: Harvard University Press, 1940.

Hansen, Marcus Lee, The Immigrant in American History. Cambridge: Harvard University Press, 1940.

Hartley, Eugene L., Problems in Prejudice. New York: King's Crown Press, 1946.

Haynor, Norman, and Charles Reynold, "Chinese Family Life in America," American Sociological Review, 2 (October, 1937), pp. 630-637.

Higham, John, Strangers in the Land: Patterns of American Nativism, 1860-1925. New Brunswick: Rutgers University Press, 1955.

Hill, Herbert, "Anti-Oriental Agitation and the Rise of Workingclass Racism," Society, X, No. 2 (January-February, 1973), pp. 43-54.

Hoffman, James W. (ed.), Concerns of a Continent. New York: Friendship Press, 1958.

Hoy, William, The Chinese Six Companies. San Francisco: The Chinese Consolidated Benevolent Association, 1942.

Hsu, Francis L.K., Americans and Chinese--Two Ways of Life. New York: Henry Schuman, 1953.

Hsu, Francis L.K., The Challenge of the American Dreams: The Chinese in the United States. Belmont, Calif.: Wadsworth Publishing Co., 1971.

Hsu, Francis L.K., Under the Ancestor's Shadow. New York: Columbia University Press, 1948.

Hsu, Francis L.K., "What Americans Need to Know About China," Asia, 45 (March, 1945), pp. 129-132.

Hsu, Kai-yu and Helen Palubinski, Asian American Authors. Boston:

Houghton Mifflin Co., 1972.

Huang, Foo-luan, Hua-Ch'iao Yu Chung Kuo Ke Ming (The Overseas Chinese and the Chinese Revolution). Hongkong: Asia Publishing Co., 1954.

Huang, Tsen-ming, The Legal Status of the Chinese Abroad. Taipei, Taiwan: China Cultural Service, 1954.

Hunt, Rockwell (ed.), California and the Californians. Chicago: G. W. Lewis Publishing Co., 1926.

Hwuy, Ung, A Chinaman's Opinion of Us and of His Own People. New York: Frederick A. Stokes & Co., 1927.

Invalidity of the "Queue Ordinance" of the City and County of San Francisco, The. San Francisco: J.L. Rice & Co., 1879.

Irwin, William Henry, Old Chinatown. New York: M. Kennerley, 1913.

Isaacs, H.R., Scratches on Our Minds: American Images of China and India. New York: John Day, 1958.

Iyenaga, Toyokichi, "Discrimination with Reference to Citizenship and Land Ownership," Proceedings of the Academy of Political Science, 7 (July, 1917), pp. 565-569.

Jacobs, Paul, and Saul Landau, with Eve Pell, To Serve the Devil, Vol. II: Colonials and Sojourners. New York: Random House, 1971.

Javits, Jacob, Discrimination--U.S.A. New York: Harcourt, Brace, & World, 1960.

Jenks, Jeremiah W., and W. Jett Lauck (eds.), The Immigration Problem: A Study of American Immigration Conditions and Needs (6th ed.). New York: Funk & Wagnalls Co., 1926.

Johnson, Emory R., "Chinese and Japanese in America," The Annals of the Academy of Political and Social Science, XXXIV, No. 2 (September, 1909), pp. 1-203.

Jones, Dorothy, The Portrayal of China and India on the American Screen, 1896-1955. Cambridge: MIT, Center for International Studies, 1955

Karlin, Jules Alexander, "The Anti-Chinese Outbreaks in Seattle, 1885-1886," The Pacific Northwest Quarterly, XXXIX, No. 2 (April, 1948), pp. 103-130.

Kinnear, George, Anti-Chinese Riots in Seattle, February 8, 1886. Seattle: George Kinnear, 1911.

Klineberg, Otto, Race and Psychology (UNESCO Publication No. 842). Paris, 1951.

Kohler, Max J., Immigration and Aliens in the United States. New York: Bloch Publishing Co., 1936.

Konvitz, Milton R., The Alien and the Asiatic in American Law. Ithaca: Cornell University Press, 1946.

Konvitz, Milton R., Civil Rights in Immigration. Ithaca: Cornell University Press, 1946.

Kung, S.W., Chinese in American Life. Seattle: University of Washington Press, 1962.

Kuznets, Simon, and Ernest Rubin, Immigration and the Foreign Born (Occasional Paper, No. 46). New York: National Bureau of Economic Research, 1954.

Kwoh, Beulah Ong, "The Occupational Status of American-Born Chinese Male College Graduates," American Journal of Sociology, LIII, No. 3 (November, 1947), pp. 192-200.

Laki, Verge, and Pauli Murray (eds.), States' Laws on Race and Color and Appendices. Cincinnati: Woman's Division of Christian Service, Board of Missions of the Methodist Church Service Center, 1950; Supplement, 1955.

Lang, Olga, Chinese Family and Society. New Haven: Yale University Press, 1946.

LaPiere, Richard T., "Attitudes vs. Actions," Social Forces, XIII, No. 2 (December, 1934), pp. 230-237.

Lasker, Bruno, Race Attitudes in Children. New York: Henry Holt & Co., 1929.

Laughlin, H.H., Immigration and Conquest. New York: Chamber of Commerce of the State of New York, 1939.

Layres, Augustus, Both Sides of Chinese Question; Critical Analysis of the Evidence for and against Chinese Immigration, as Elicited before the Congressional Commission. San Francisco: Woodbridge Printer, 1877.

Lee, Calvin, Chinatown, USA, A History and Guide. Garden City, N.Y.: Doubleday, 1965.

Lee, Chingwah, "The Second Generation of the Chinese," Hospital Social Service, XXI (March, 1930), pp. 192-197.

Lee, Rose Hum, "Chinese Immigration and Population Changes Since 1940," Sociology and Social Research, 41 (January, 1957), pp. 195-202.

Lee, Rose Hum, The Chinese in the United States of America. Hongkong: Hongkong University Press, 1960.

Lee, Rose Hum, "The Decline of Chinatown in the United States," American Journal of Sociology, LIV, No. 5 (March, 1949), pp. 422-432.

Lee, Rose Hum, "Delinquent, Neglected and Dependent Chinese Boys and Girls of the San Francisco Bay Region," Journal of Social Psychology, XXXVI, 1st half (August, 1952), pp. 15-34.

Lee, Rose Hum, "Established Chinese Families of the San Francisco Bay Area," Midwest Sociologist, 20 (December, 1957), pp. 19-26.

Lee, Samuel D., San Francisco's Chinatown. San Francisco: National Youth Administration, 1940.

Lee, W.J., "Chinese Studies in America," Free China Review, October, 1966, pp. 31-38.

Lin, Yueh-hwa, The Golden Wing: A Sociological Study of Chinese Familism. New York: Oxford University Press, 1947.

Lin, Yutang, Chinatown Family. New York: John Day, 1948.

Lind, Andrew W., Hawaii's People. Honolulu: University of Hawaii Press, 1955.

Lind, Andrew W., An Island Community: Ecological Succession in Hawaii. Chicago: Chicago University Press, 1938.

Ling, Pyau, "Causes of Chinese Emigration," The Annals of the American Academy of Political and Social Science, XXXIX (January, 1912), pp. 74-82.

Liu, Chiang, "Chinese Versus American Ideas Concerning the Family," Journal of Applied Sociology, X (1925-1926), pp. 243-248.

Liu, Kwang-ching, Americans and Chinese. Cambridge: Harvard University Press, 1963.

Liu, Ling, Chinese in North America (in Chinese), 1949.

Loewen, James W., The Mississippi Chinese. Cambridge: Harvard University Press, 1971.

Lorden, Doris M., "The Chinese Hawaiian Family," American Journal of Sociology, XL, No. 4 (January, 1935), pp. 453-463.

Louis, K.K., "Problems of Second Generation Chinese," Sociology and Social Research, XVI (January-February, 1932), pp. 455-462.

Lowenstein, Edith, The Alien and the Immigration Law. New York: Oceana Publications, 1958.

Lui, Garding, Inside Los Angeles Chinatown. Los Angeles: Garding Lui, 1948.

Lung, C.F., "A Chinese Student and Western Culture," Sociology and Social Research, 16 (November, 1931), pp. 23-38.

Lush, H.H., "Real Yellow Peril," North American Review, 186 (November, 1907), pp. 375-383.

Lyman, Stanford M., The Asians in the West. Reno, Nevada: Desert Research Institute, 1970.

McClellan, Robert, The Heathen Chinese. Columbus: Ohio State University Press, 1971.

McEntire, Davis, Residence and Race. Berkeley: University of California Press, 1960.

McKenzie, R.D., Oriental Exclusion. Chicago: University of Chicago Press, 1928.

McKenzie, R.D., "The Oriental Finds a Job," Survey, LVI (May, 1926), pp. 151-153, 218, 221.

McKenzie, R.D., "The Oriental Invasion," Journal of Applied Sociology, X (November-December, 1925), pp. 120-130.

McLeod, Alexander, Pigtail and Gold Dust. Idaho: Caxton Printers, 1871.

MacNair, Harley Farnsworth, The Chinese Abroad: Their Position and
Protection, A Study in International Law and Relations. Shanghai: Commercial Press, 1924.

Maney, E.S., "New Trends in American Immigration," Department of
State Bulletin, XXX, No. 773 (April 19, 1954), pp. 599-602.

Mar, Dave, I Am Yellow (Curious). Davis, Calif.: University of California Asian American Research Project, 1969.

Marden, Charles F., Minorities in American Society. New York: American Book Co., 1952.

Margo, Elizabeth, Taming the Forty-Niner. New York: Rinehart & Co.,
1955.

Markham, Edwin, California, the Wonderful. New York: Hearst's International, 1914.

Maurice, Davie, World Immigration. New York: Macmillan Co., 1936.

McWilliams, C., California, the Great Exception. New York: Current
Books, 1949.

McWilliams C., "Racism on the West Coast," New Republic, 110 (May 29,
1944), pp. 732-733.

Mears, Eliot Grinnell, Resident Orientals on the American Pacific Coast;
Their Legal and Economic Status. Chicago: University of Chicago
Press, 1928.

Memmi, Albert, The Colonizer and the Colonized. New York: Orion
Press, 1965.

Miller, Stuart C., The Unwelcome Immigrant: the American Image of the
Chinese, 1785-1882. Berkeley: University of California Press, 1969.

Molloy, Timothy J., "A Century of Chinese Immigration: A Brief Review,"
Monthly Review (United States Immigration and Naturalization Service),
V., No. 6 (December, 1947), pp. 69-74.

Murphey, Rhoads, "Boston's Chinatown," Economic Geography, XXVIII,
No. 3 (July, 1952), pp. 245-255.

Nash, Gary B., and Richard Weiss, The Great Fear: Race in the Mind of
America. New York: Holt, Rinehart & Winston, 1970.

New York Cinese Laundry Social Athletic Club, Inc., Special Issue. New York, 1972.

Norr, William, Stories of Chinatown. Sketches from Life in the Chinese Colony of Mott, Pell and Doyers Streets. New York: W. Norr, 1892.

Norton, Henry K., The Story of California. Chicago: A.C. McClurg & Co., 1913.

Nutting, H.C., "Immigration from the Orient," Nation, 98 (June 18, 1914), pp. 724-725.

O'Brien, Herbert W., "Status of Chinese in Mississippi Delta," Social Force, 20 (March, 1941), pp. 386-390.

Ouarado, Patrick K., "The Chinese in Colorado," Colorado Magazine, XXIX, No. 4 (October, 1952), pp. 273-284.

Palmer, Albert W., Orientals in American Life. New York: Friendship Press, 1934.

Palmer, Phil, Chinatown, San Francisco. Berkeley: Howell-North, 1960.

Panunzio, Constantine, "Intermarriage in Los Angeles, 1924-1933," American Journal of Sociology, XLVII, No. 5 (March, 1942), pp. 690-701.

Panunzio, Constantine, The Soul of An Immigrant. New York: Macmillan Co., 1921.

Park, No Yong, Chinaman's Chance. Boston: Meador Press, 1940.

Park, No Yong, An Oriental View of American Civilization. Boston & New York: Hale, Cushman & Flint, 1934.

Park, Robert E., "A Race Relations Study of Oriental Population of the Pacific Coast," Journal of Applied Sociology, 8 (March, 1924), pp. 195-205.

Patterson, R., "Tongs in San Francisco," American Mercury, 74 (February, 1952), pp. 93-99.

People's Foreign Relations Association of China, The, Handbook of Chinese in America (in Chinese), 1946.

Peters, C.A., Immigration Problem (Reference Shelf, Vol. XIX, No. 7). New York: H.W. Wilson Co., 1948.

Phelps, Harold A., and David Henderson, Population in Its Human Aspect. New York: Appleton-Century-Crofts, 1958.

"Private Bills and Immigration," Harvard Law Review, LXIX, No. 6 (April, 1956), pp. 1083-1096.

Prothro, E. Terry, and Otha King Miles, "Social Distance in the Deep South as Measured by a Revised Bogardus Scale," Journal of Social Psychology, XXXVII, 2nd half (May, 1953), pp. 171-174.

Pruitt, Ida, The Daughter of Han. New Haven: Yale University Press, 1945.

Reit, Seymour (photographs by Paul Conklin), Ricecake and Paper Dragons. New York: Dodd, Mead & Co., 1973.

Remer, C.F., A Study of Chinese Boycott with Special Reference to Their Economic Effectiveness. Baltimore: Johns Hopkins Press, 1933.

Report of the Commission on Race and Housing, Where Shall We Live. Berkeley: University of California Press, 1949.

Report on World Population Migrations. Washington, D.C.: George Washington University Press, 1956.

Rhodes, James Ford, History of the United States from the Compromise of 1850 to the McKinley-Bryan Campaign of 1896, 8 vols. New York: Macmillan Co., 1920.

Riggs, Fred W., Pressures on Congress: A Study of the Repeal of Chinese Exclusion. New York: King's Crown Press, 1950.

Ritchie, R.W., "The Wars of the Tongs," Harper's Weekly, 54 (August 27, 1910), pp. 8-10.

Ritter, Edward, Helen Ritter, and Stanley Spector, Americans All, Our Oriental Americans. New York: McGraw-Hill, 1965.

Rohmer, Sax, Tales of Chinatown. New York: Doubleday, Page & Co., 1922.

Rose, Arnold, and Caroline Rose, America Divided. New York: Alfred A. Knopf, 1955.

Ross, Edward A., The Changing Chinese, the Conflict of Oriental and Western Cultures in China. New York: Century Co., 1911.

Sabin, Edwin L., Building the Pacific Railway. Philadelphia: J.B. Lippen-
cott Co., 1919.

Sakai, Joyce and David Mar (eds.), Asians in America: Selected Student
Papers. Davis, Calif.: University of California Press, 1970.

Sandmeyer, Elmer Clarence, The Anti-Chinese Movement in California.
Urbana, Illinois: University of Illinois Press, 1939.

Sandmeyer, Elmer Clarence, "California Anti-Chinese Legislation and the
Federal Courts: A Study in Federal Relations," Pacific Historical Review, V, No. 3 (September, 1936), pp. 189-211.

Saniford, P., and R. Kerr, "Intelligence of Chinese and Japanese Children,"
Journal of Educational Psychology, 17 (1926), pp. 361-367.

Saxton, Alexander Plaisted, The Indispensable Enemy; Labor and the Anti-
Chinese Movement in California. Berkeley: University of California
Press, 1971.

Schermerhorn, Richard A., These Our People: Minorities in American
Culture. Boston: D.C. Heath & Co., 1949.

Schrieke, B., Alien Americans: A Study of Race Relations. New York:
Viking Press, 1936.

Schwartz, Shepard, "Mate-Selecting Among New York City's Chinese
Males, 1931-1938," American Journal of Sociology, LVI, No. 6 (May,
1951), pp. 562-568.

Selvin, David F., The Other San Francisco. New York: Seabury Press,
1969.

"Seventh Semi-Annual Report of the Administrator of the Refugee Act of
1953 as Amended," Interpreter Releases, XXXIV, No. 7 (February 27,
1957), pp. 40-42.

Seward, George F., Chinese Immigration in Its Social and Economic Aspects. New York: Charles Scribner & Sons, 1881.

Shaw, William, Golden Dreams and Waking Realities; Being the Adventures
of a Gold-Seeker in California and the Pacific Islands. London: Smith,
Elder & Co., 1851.

Sidney, Kansas, Immigration and the Nationality Act (Annotated with Rules
and Regulations). New York: Immigrations Publications, 1953.

Sidney, Kansas, 1954-1959 Cumulative Supplement to Fourth Edition of
Immigration and Nationality Act. Buffalo: Dennis & Co., 1959.

Sifakis, C., "Last Great Tong War," Coronet (March, 1958), pp. 60-64.

Simpson, George Eaton, and J. Milton Yinger, Racial and Cultural Minorities. New York: Harper & Brothers, 1953.

Smith, William C., Americans in Process. Ann Arbor, Mich.: J.W.
Edwards, 1937.

Smith, William C., The Second Generation Oriental in America. Honolulu:
Institute of Pacific Relations, 1927.

Spinks, Nelson, "Repeal Chinese Exclusion," Asia and the Americans, 42
(February, 1942), pp. 92-94.

Statusz-Hupe, Robert (ed.), American-Asian Tensions (Foreign Policy Research Institute Series No. 3). New York: Frederick A. Praeger, 1956.

Stephenson, George M., A History of American Immigration, 1820-1924.
Boston: Ginn & Co., 1926.

Sung, Betty Lee, Mountain of Gold: The Story of Chinese in America.
New York: Macmillan Co., 1967.

Survey of Chinese Students in American Universities and Colleges in the
Past Hundred Years, A. New York: National Tsing Hua University Research Fellowship Fund and China Institute in America, 1954.

Swisher, Carl Brent, Motivation and Political Technique in the California
Constitutional Convention, 1878-1879. Claremont, Calif.: Pomona
College, 1930.

Tachiki, Amy, Eddie Wong, Franklin Odo, with Buck Wong (eds.), Roots:
An Asian American Reader. Los Angeles: UCLA Asian American Studies Center, 1971.

Taft, Donald, Human Migration: A Study of International Movements.
New York: Ronald Press, 1936.

Thomas, Brinley (ed.), Economics of International Migration (Proceedings
of a Conference Held by the International Economic Association). London:
Macmillan Co., 1958.

Thompson, Warren S., Growth and Changes in California's Population.

Los Angeles: Haynes Foundation, 1955.

Thurstone, L. L., "The Measurement of Change in Social Attitude,"
Journal of Social Psychology, II, No. 2 (May, 1931), pp. 230-235.

Tow, Julius Su, The Real Chinese in America. Orange, N.J.: Academy
Press, 1923.

Tsu, Hsu-hsieh (ed.), Hua-ch'iao Tze (The Chinese in Foreign Countries).
Taipei, Taiwan: Overseas Publishing Co., 1956.

Tung, William L., China and the Foreign Powers. Dobbs Ferry, N.Y.:
Oceana Publications, 1970.

Tyler, Poyntz (ed.), Immigration and the United States (Reference Shelf,
Vol. XXVIII, No. 1), New York: H.W. Wilson Co., 1956.

Uchida, Naosaku (ed.), The Overseas Chinese: A Bibliographical Essay
Based on the Resources of the Hoover Institution. Stanford: Stanford
University Press, 1959.

Van Vleck, William C., The Administrative Control of Aliens. New York:
The Commonwealth Fund, 1958.

Villard, O.G., "Justice for the Chinese," Christian Century, 60 (May 26,
1943), pp. 633-634.

Von Kaltenborn, Hans, "Land Ownership by Aliens," Proceedings of the
Academy of Political Science, 7 (July, 1917), pp. 570-575.

Wagley, Charles, and Marvin Harris, Minorities in the New World. New
York: Columbia University Press, 1958.

Waln, Nora, House of Exile. New York: Blue Ribbon Books, 1933.

Wang, Gung Hsing, The Chinese Mind. New York: John Day, 1946.

Warner, W. Lloyd, and Leo Srole, The Social Systems of American
Ethnic Groups. New Haven: Yale University Press, 1949.

Wellborn, Mildred, "The Events Leading to the Chinese Exclusion Acts,"
Historical Society of Southern California, Annual Publications, IX (1914)
pp. 49-58.

Wheaton, Donald W., "Spotlights on the Political History of California
from 1887 to 1898," California Historical Society Quarterly, V, No. 3

(September, 1926), pp. 283-288.

Whiteside, T., "Wet Wash Chinatown," New Republic, 115 (December 23, 1946), pp. 872-874.

Whitney, James A., The Chinese and the Chinese Question. New York: Tibbals Book Co., 1888.

Wilcox, W.P., "Anti-Chinese Riots in Washington," Washington Historical Quarterly, XX, No. 3 (July, 1929), pp. 204-211.

Williams, Frederick Wells, Anson Burlingame and the First Chinese Mission to Foreign Powers. New York: Charles Scribner & Sons, 1912.

Williams, Stephen, The Chinese in the California Mines, 1848-1860. Stanford: R. & E. Research Associates, 1971.

Wittke, C.F., We Who Build America. New York: Prentice-Hall, 1939.

Wollenberg, Charles, Ethnic Conflict in California History. Los Angeles: Tinnon-Brown, 1970.

Woofter, T.J., Races and Ethnic Groups in American Life. New York: McGraw-Hill, 1933.

Wu, Cheng-tsu (ed.), "Chink!" A Documentary History of Anti-Chinese Prejudice in America. New York: World Publishing Co., 1972.

Wu, S.Y., One Hundred Years of Chinese in the United States and Canada. Hongkong: S.Y. Wu, 1954.

Yeung, K.T., "The Intelligence of Chinese Children," Journal of Applied Psychology, V (1922), pp. 267-274.

Young, Donald R., American Minority Peoples: A Study in Racial and Cultural Conflicts in the United States. New York: Harper & Brothers, 1932.

Young, P.V., "Support of the Anti-Oriental Movement," The Annals of the American Academy of Political and Social Science, 34 (September, 1909), pp. 231-238.

Yung, Wing, My Life in China and America. New York: Henry Holt & Co., 1909.

Ziegler, B.M., Immigration, An American Dilemma. Boston: D.C. Heath & Co., 1953.

APPENDIX

APPENDIX

Chinese Organizations in Washington, D.C. and Several American Cities with Large Chinese Population

Washington, D.C.

Chinese Consolidated Benevolent Association

Kuomintang of China

Min Chee Tang

On Leong Chinese Merchants Association

Hip Sing Association

Lee's Benevolent Association

Lee King Shu Club

Chew Lun Association

Moy's Association

Gee How Oak Tin Association

Yee Fun Toy Hong

Wong's Association

Eng's Association

Lung Kong Tin Yee Association

Yeng Kiang Association

Lun Hing Club

Chinese American Citizens Alliance, Washington, D.C. Lodge

D.C. Chinese Senior Citizens Club, Inc.

Chinese Medical and Health Association

Chinese Christian Church

Overseas Chinese Youth Club

Jow Ga Kung Fu Association

Chinese Youth Club

Sing Ping Musical Club

Chinese Community Church

New York City

Chinese Consolidated Benevolent Association

Hoy Sun Ling Yeung Benevolent Association

Min Chih Tang

Kuomintang Branch Office

Tsung Tsin Association

Lung Kong Tin Yee Association

Chung San Association

Tung On Association

Hok San Society

G.H. Oak Tin Association

Eng Suey Sun Association

Lee's Family Association

Wong Family Benevolent
  Association

Chee Tuck San Tuck Association

Moy's Family Association

Sun Wei Association

Nam Sun Club

Yee Fong Toy Association

Tai Pun Association

Chinese Laundry Association

Chow Lun Association

Soo Yuen Association

Sam Yick Association

Loung Chung How Tong

Yee Shan Benevolent
  Society

Chinese Community Club

Chee Yue Community Association

Lun Sai Ho Association

Kwong Hoy Association

Cuban Chinese Refugee
  Association

New York Chinese Import &
  Export Association

New York Chinese Garment
  Maker Association

Lin Sing Association

Chinese Merchant's Association

Hip Sing Association

Chinese Chamber of Commerce, Inc.

Hoy Yin Association

Sze Kong Mutual Benevolent Association

Fay Chow Merchant's Association

Chinese American Restaurant Association

Lun Yee Association

The American Legion, Chinese Memorial
  Post 1291

Chinese Women's Benevolent Association

Hoy Ping Association

Chinese Musical & Theatrical Association

Tai Look Merchant's Association

Hainan Association

Fukien Association

The First Chinese Presbyterian Church

Chinese Dramatic & Benevolent
  Association

National Chinese Seamen's Union, Inc.

San Kiang Charitable Association

Wah Pei Association

Tseng Sun Sing Association

Yan Ping Gong Yee

Gee Poy Kuo Association

Fonn Lun Benevolent Association

Yuen's Association

Chinese American Citizens Alliance

Chinese Cultural Renaissance Society

Institute of Chinese Culture

China Institute in America, Inc.

Sino-American Amity

National Federation for Chinese
  Culture and Heritage, Inc.

San Francisco

Chinese Consolidated Benevolent Association

Ning Yung Benevolent
  Association

Sue Hing Benevolent Asso-
  ciation

Hop Wo Benevolent Association

Kong Chow Benevolent
  Association

Young Wo Benevolent
  Association

Sam Yup Benevolent Association

Yan Wo Benevolent Association

Chinese Chamber of Commerce

Chinese-American Citizens Alliance

Chinese Women's United Association

Tung Hwa Association

Chinese Culture Association

Chinese Culture Center

Oakland Consolidated Chinese
  Association

Berkeley Chinese Center

Honolulu

United Chinese Society

Associated Chinese University Women

Buck Toy Club

Kutt Hing Society

Leong Doo Society

Lin Yee Chung Association

Cha Yun Wai Pok Sha

Chee How Oak Tin Benevolent Society

Chinese Buddhist Association of
  Hawaii

Chinese Christian Association of
  Hawaii

Chinese Literature & Arts Association of Hawaii

Chinese Women's Club

Ching Wan Musical & Dramatic Club

Chun Wing Chin Tong

Council of the Chinese Culture
  Renaissance--Hawaii Chapter

Goo Clan

Hawaii Chinese Buddhist Society

Hawaii Chinese Educational
  Association

Honolulu Chinese Jaycees

Hoo Cho Sha Society

Kau Tom Post No. 11

Kong Chau Society

Kung Sheong Doo Society

Lukes of Hawaii

Lung Doo Chung Sing Tong

Lung Tao Wan Villagers' Club

Mau Club of Hawaii

See Dai Doo Society

Sheong Gar Hong Society

Sun Ming Ting Association

Tan Sing Dramatic Club

Tsung Tsin Association

United Church of Christ

Wong Kong Har Tong

Yee Yi Tong

American Chinese Club

Au Clan

Chang Wing Young Tong

Chee Kung Tong Society

Chinese Catholic Club

Chinese Chamber of Commerce
  of Hawaii

Chinese Cultural Foundation of Hawaii

Chinese Physical Culture Association

Chinese Social Club

Ching Benevolent Society of Hawaii

Choy Hung Village Club

Chung Shan Association

Duck Doo Society

Free China Women's Relief Society

Gook Doo Sam Heong

Hawaii Chinese Civic Association

Hawaii Chinese History Center

Hee Gow Yong Tong

Ho Society

Kam Society

Ket On Society

Kong Tow Society

Kuo Min Tang Society

Lee Association

Leong Soong Duck Tong

Ling How Pang Society

Lum Sai Ho Tong

Lung Kong Kung Shaw Society

Mandarin Club of Hawaii

On Tong Tung Heong Society

See Yup Benevolent Society

Shue Yuen Quon Chack Shai

Tai Chi Physical Culture Association

Tom Association

United Chinese Labor Association

Wai Sin Wui Club

Wong Leong Doo Chuck Sing Tong

Young Association

INDEX